When Prince Charming
Falls off His Horse

When Prince Charming falls off his horse

Jerry and Judy Schreur
with Jack Schreur

Chariot VICTOR
PUBLISHING
A DIVISION OF COOK COMMUNICATIONS

Victor Books is an imprint of ChariotVictor Publishing,
a division of Cook Communications, Colorado Springs, Colorado 80918
Cook Communications, Paris, Ontario
Kingsway Communications, Eastbourne, England

Schruer, Jerry, 1941–
    When Prince Charming falls off his horse / Jerry and Judy Schreur
    with Jack Schreur
        p. cm.
    ISBN 1-56476-628-4
    1. Married people—United States—Psychology. 2. Man–woman
    relationships—United States. 3. Commitment (Psychology). 4. Intimacy
    (Psychology). I. Schreur, Judy. II. Schreur, Jack, 1964–   . III. Title.
    HQ734.S395   1997
    306.872—dc21   97-36294
                                                                                                              CIP

Most Scripture is from the *Holy Bible, New International Version*®. Copyright © 1973,
1978, 1984 by International Bible Society. Used by permission of Zondervan Publishing
House. All rights reserved; other references are from the *Authorized (King James)
Version.*

Editing: Jerry Yamamoto and Barbara Williams
Design: Bill Gray
Cover Illustration: Linn W. Trochim

1 2 3 4 5 6 7 8 9 10 Printing/Year 01 00 99 98 97

To Perk and Mary Hamming

Thank you for more than thirty years of friendship.

Thank you for coming alongside of a rebellious young couple

to point us to Jesus. Because of your influence we are called

"children of God,"

because of your influence we are in ministry today,

because of your influence we are celebrating

thirty-three years of marriage. We love you guys! This book is for you.

We hope it will touch other lives as you have touched ours.

contents

CHAPTER I

The Romantic Ideal

he awoke with a start. It was an unfamiliar room. Where was she? Slowly the realization crept in; she was married, and she had found Prince Charming. The week leading up to the wedding had been a blur for Cinderella. First the business with her fairy godmother, then the great dance and the hurried departure. She had left her glass slipper, and he had tracked her down. It was so romantic, and he was so handsome in those cute tights, sitting on that white horse. And had her stepmother and stepsisters been angry—and so very jealous! With a contented sigh, Cinderella remembered the king as very kind and her Prince as gallant and gentle. He was everything she had dreamed of. Up until now her life had been difficult and filled with drudgery, but now it would be an unending delight. Love and affection would fill her soul, and the insecurities that had plagued her and the desperation she had felt on losing her mother and father all would fade away, because she had found true love. A loud noise broke *her reverie, then a snort followed by an odd gurgling sound. Turning her lovely golden head, she saw her sweet prince. Evidently (and this she wasn't prepared for), Prince Charming snored, and even more disgusting, he was drooling. Stroking his hair, she let her eyes glance around the room. She had never lived in a castle before. It was all so grand, and so (well, as she shivered and tried to pull the covers closer around her), kind of drafty too. And dark. Smiling at his snores and trying to ignore the wet spot on the pillow, Cinderella drifted back into a less contented sleep. Surely, she thought, here is where they write "and they all lived happily ever after."*

They were alone in the room, and the only light was the blue glow of the TV set. Predictably, he was sleeping; and predictably, she was crying. The movie had reached its moment of truth: Cary Grant turned and saw her looking his way; he ran to her; they embraced; their lips met; they kissed hungrily; and then the credits rolled. Barbara pushed her sleeping husband as she tried to blow her nose. "Hey, it's time to go to bed. The movie's over. Let's go." With a groan he rose to his feet and stumbled into their bed and back to sleep without a word to his wife. Shaking her head at his comatose form, Barbara lay awake for a long time. Her life hadn't exactly turned out as she had planned. After ten years of marriage, the spark was gone, and the excitement that once burned through her every time she thought of him had long ago become a rather amused tolerance. Now, lying in bed, she realizes that she's profoundly disappointed. The fairy tale is over. Her husband never looks at her the way Cary Grant looked at Rosalind Russell. For that matter, she never looks at him that way either. Barbara thinks of all the fairy tales she's seen on the silver screen, of all the novels that ended with happily ever after, and the question insistently refuses to go away. What happens then? After the credits roll, after the last page is turned, after they ride off into the sunset, what happens then? With a rueful smile that reroutes the tears, Barbara asks, "What happens when Prince Charming falls off his horse?"

Barbara's question is a good one. In fact, it's a question that every married person asks at one time or another. We see a lot of fairy tales, and they all end the same way—the kiss and the ride into some imagined perfect future. But what really happens after that? The truth is that real life is 98 percent "what happened then." And the popular culture that feeds our dreams and ideals doesn't prepare us very well for that 98 percent. We know in our heads that bells and whistles won't go off every time we kiss our husband or wife for the rest of our lives. We know in our heads that there will be times when the toothpaste is rolled up the wrong way or the dirty underwear is left on the floor. We may even be so prescient as to think that there will be moments when the spark is gone and it will take strong commitment to stay married. But rarely do we understand the sheer boredom that can come with ten or twenty years of marriage. It is a prophet of sorts who can see the silent dinner table that afflicts many of our homes because we have just run out of things to say to each other. That is what takes so many of us by surprise. We are prepared for clothes on the floor and minor irritations, but the boredom and lack of interest surprise us, and the wear of everyday life takes its own toll on our marriage.

When Sheila and Dave walked into my office, they held hands, but it wasn't an act of tenderness to touch. They were holding on for dear life, as if letting go of each other risked losing "touch" forever. They were scared, worried, and very ready to talk. "I don't know what happened. It's like everything he does bugs me. I still say I love him, but more and more the words are empty and all the feelings behind them are gone. I say it now out of habit, not because I still mean it." He was no less sparing: "Honestly, I don't find her interesting or attractive. Sexually we are dead, and I don't really even miss it that much. We don't share the same interests; all we seem to have to talk about are the kids. We've been married for fifteen years, and I don't know how much longer we can keep this up." Together, still clenching hands, they say, "Jerry we made our vows for life, and we want to live up to them, but it seems so empty. What can we do?"

Sheila and Dave were more honest than most of the couples I've counseled, and they certainly laid it on the line faster than most, but their struggle and their words have been replayed countless times in front of me. We want to be in love; we want to stay married; we want to live up to our vows; but after a while, be it five, ten, or twenty years, it just seems too hard. And everything else, everything except being married to this person, begins to look very good.

As a pastoral counselor I help prepare hundreds of young couples for marriage. I also counsel hundreds of couples on the brink of ending their marriages. I see the hopes, dreams, and expectations of people in love, and I see the despair, betrayal, and anger of couples on the brink of divorce. I speak to men and women who are on their third or even fourth marriage, trying to figure out what went wrong and how to fix it. I hear from nervous brides and grooms who wonder how they can avoid the fate of their parents and so many of their friends. Falling in love is easy, and getting married perhaps even easier, but staying happily married, or for that matter staying married at all, is an entirely different and much more difficult thing.

Of course, I'm not just a counselor. I'm also a husband and a father.

Judy and I have been married for over thirty years, and I'm sure she agrees with me when I admit that most of them were happy years. We've watched two sons walk down the aisle, eyes shining with love. We walked the tough road of divorce with one of those sons, eyes now brimming with tears and disappointment. I believe in marriage, but I also believe it can be tough. And in our society the unrealistic expectations we place on couples and the unwarranted emphasis we place on romance makes marriage even tougher.

I believe that when two people commit to their marriage, they can work through almost any difficulty, overcome almost any obstacle, and find a happy, enjoyable marriage. I don't believe that many of us will find a love that fulfills all of our needs and desires. I don't believe many of us will be "in love" in the romantic sense for a lifetime. And I think that anyone who tells you differently is setting you up for failure and disappointment. It is always possible to be more intimate in your marriage and to find more effective means of communication and more romantic ways of expressing your love. It is not possible to be totally and completely intimate all the time, to communicate effectively every minute of every day, and to live up to our society's romantic ideal month after month and year after year.

This book is about truth. You won't find ten steps to a perfect marriage in this book. You won't hear a magic formula, and we promise no magic wands to wipe away years of hurt or to undo poor choices from the past. What you will find in the following pages is the wisdom of the survivors, the knowledge that comes only with years of trying and failing and trying again. I believe that you will also find hope, because in these pages we are going to be realistic about what you can and cannot expect. Yet we also hold out the belief that your marriage can be the single most

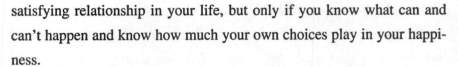

satisfying relationship in your life, but only if you know what can and can't happen and know how much your own choices play in your happiness.

I guess there's no better way to get started than to talk about our life and how our marriage got its start thirty-three years ago. Our story is a cautionary one, yet it ultimately has a happy ending. In our experiences, you may see your own life. My wife Judy is the better storyteller by far, and I'll let her words guide you through the next pages.

I knew his reputation and had heard about Jerry Schreur long before I met him. Rumors and facts were hard to separate, but he was a talked-about guy. Jerry Schreur—thief, hood, motorcycle rider with his black leather jacket and sideburns. He was allegedly the toughest guy in our little town. People said, "When he was arrested, the police never went alone."

His driving record filled an eight and a half-inch sheet of paper—single spaced! The offenses included careless driving, speeding, and attempting to outrun the police. Many times these chases included speeds well over one hundred miles an hour. His major goal in life was to outsmart, annoy, and harass the local law enforcement officers. There were wild parties with drinking and sex. He became a regular resident of the county jail. I remember hearing on the news and reading in the newspaper the announcement of his arrest for breaking and entering. I knew people were afraid of him because of his reputation for fighting. He also liked driving around with a broken down shotgun in the rear window of his car for all to see.

I remember sitting in the backseat of my mother's 1952

Chevy; my sister Jan was at my side. My aunt was sitting in the front with my mother. Jerry flew past us at really high speed. "Humph, there goes that Jerry Schreur. They say his parents can't do a thing with him, and the police are afraid of him." (It had to be true since my neighbor was a policeman, and Mom always got the scoop from his wife.) My heart pounded; to me he seemed just perfect! Hudsonville's very own version of James Dean and *Rebel without a Cause*! Then came that fateful day in May. I was 15 years old and working in the local root beer stand. It was a hangout for some of the "cool" kids in the area. It had everything I could want: pinball machines, a jukebox, hamburgers, fries, malts, and lots of guys for me to flirt with. My definition of the perfect job. Jerry came roaring up on a motorcycle, complete with a black leather jacket and sideburns. When he walked in, the sun shone behind him, and all I could see was a dark shadow of a six-foot frame. (WOW, just like the movies.) I took one look at him and thought, "That's Jerry Schreur, and I'm going to show all those Baptists that I can go with him, the worst and most notorious guy in town."

For the first time in my life I was going to be somebody. I was going to be Jerry Schreur's girlfriend. My girlfriend and I worked out a plan. Whenever Jerry would come in, I would serve him. I did the same for her when the guy she wanted came in. Jerry never caught on, and we became friends. One evening I told my mom she didn't have to pick me up because my friend would take me home. I "happened" to mention to Jerry that I didn't have a ride home that night because my mom needed the car and couldn't pick me up. He offered to take me, and I sweetly accepted.

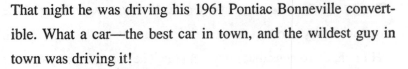

That night he was driving his 1961 Pontiac Bonneville convertible. What a car—the best car in town, and the wildest guy in town was driving it!

That night was the beginning of a wild crazy ride. He took me home, and we talked for a long time in the yard. It was Thursday night, and he asked me for a date the next night. Of course, I accepted. As he leaned over to kiss me, I innocently looked at him and said, "Oh, no. I don't kiss on the first date," thinking all the time, "OK, you look good, Judy. I hope he tries again." I don't think I'll tell you if he did.

On our first real date we put the top down and went riding around the Ottawa Beach State Park on Lake Michigan. It was a dream night. Our second date was the following Monday, which happened to be Memorial Day. He picked me up in the morning. My mother's last words to me that morning were "Stay around here and don't go too far." I smiled and said, "OK." I put on my sunglasses and my scarf, and off we drove to Chicago—175 miles away! My frame of reference of close and my mom's were slightly different. Jerry treated me like a princess. I had dated several boys before Jerry, but none held the excitement or were as good to me as he was. On that Memorial Day he bought me gifts and spent more money on me than anyone had ever spent. I didn't realize most of his money was either borrowed or the result of stealing. Jerry was on probation for breaking and entering and not supposed to leave the state. He was 19, and I was 15 (but I really was mature, just ask me). I never dated another person after that weekend. I ate, slept, and drank Jerry Schreur.

My friends thought it was great that I was dating Jerry. My

mother, however, had other thoughts and strong feelings. Jerry definitely was not any parent's ideal beau for their precious teenage daughter. But I didn't care. For the first time in my life I felt I was somebody. I was more than Judy Kay Schut, the daughter of the poor widow Henrietta Schut. Jerry seemed to be the answer to all my needs. Who was I? I was Jerry Schreur's girlfriend!

Everywhere I went I was noticed for something other than the poor cut of my clothes or with pity for being poor Henrietta's girl. I remember walking in the town drugstore when I heard some people in the next aisle say, "Look, there goes Jerry Schreur's girl." One time when I was skating, some boys grabbed me and tried to kiss me. While I was pushing them off, another boy skated by and said to them, "You have Jerry Schreur's girl there." They all jumped up and left. I brushed my clothes off and thought, "Now that is power!"

Jerry filled several areas of need in my life. I had a sense of identity; I belonged to someone, in fact, someone very important. He also was a very strong male figure in my life. I felt loved and needed. I liked the excitement of our relationship. Our dating life was never dull. Jerry still had his old friends, and often I was the only girl at the card games or bobsledding or motorcycle riding. Needless to say, my mother was less than totally thrilled that her daughter was dating the town criminal. My mother quoted the Scripture to me about not being unequally yoked together with unbelievers, and I remember visualizing taking those pages out of her Bible and cramming them down her throat. She didn't understand. I was finally somebody, and no one was going to take that away from me, not even my own mother.

I craved the excitement of being his girl and I enjoyed my newfound feelings as a sexual being, and I loved the feelings of power, strength, and closeness I had when I was with him. Looking back, I can only shake my head at my own selfishness and how desperately needy I was. When we dated, I thought we had a wonderful relationship. We did everything I wanted to do. Jerry never said no to me. It was great. I remember telling my mother that I was going to get married so no one would ever control me or tell me what to do. I would be free. I also remember telling Jerry one early morning when he was dropping me off, "Won't it be wonderful to get married? Then we'll never have to part or say good-bye. We could be in each other's arms all night!" I had real insight on marriage.

On February 28, 1964, we were married. I was 18, and Jerry was 22. We had dated three and a half years and I was pregnant. I was so excited. I was going to have his baby and we were going to live happily ever after. I was 18 and pregnant, with a convicted felon who had been out of work for several months for a husband, and I was setting up a home. We had no money for a honeymoon and lots of debt. Jerry was to start a new job the following Monday. I couldn't wait for our perfect life.

Prince Charming had come into my life. Sure he didn't wear tights. Jeans and a leather jacket were this prince's attire. Instead of a white horse, he rode a blue Triumph motorcycle, and our castle was an old, drafty, one-bedroom house in the middle of a field, but we were still going to live happily ever after.

The Romantic Ideal

Each day I meet men and women floundering in their relationships, feeling lost and confused because their marriage has fallen short of their romantic ideals. Husbands and wives the world over share the same dreams Judy had for our life together. And who can blame us? We want someone who will hold us when we are afraid, comfort us when we are sad, love us when we don't deserve it, and always give us unconditional acceptance. It isn't wrong to hope for perfect love, and it isn't wrong to work for a better marriage. Far from it! It is wrong to expect it, and it is damaging when we fall so very far short of those ideals.

Three Myths

When I first met Tracy and Will, they were a newlywed, happy, even giddy couple. They were both attractive young professionals, who were the walking and talking definition of a cute couple. The next time I saw them, it was only three years later. Yet something vital had drained out of their faces, and the lively fun that had inhabited their eyes was gone. Will confessed that Tracy didn't meet his needs, that she wasn't "there" for him, and that he needed someone to love him unconditionally. Tracy had grown up in a home without much affection, and it was difficult for her to give Will his daily dose of hugs and kisses. The litany of complaint was long, but it boiled down to one simple thing: Neither was meeting the other's romantic ideal. After a few years of marriage, the romance was gone. Tracy and Will had been to seminars and had read books, but they had walked away feeling even more defeated. After trying the ten steps to an intimate, affair-proof marriage, Will felt more certain than ever that he had married the wrong person. After trying unsuccessfully to be Will's best friend and intimate confidant, Tracy was at the end of her rope, wondering what to do next. As we talked, I discovered that Will and Tracy had become victims to three myths that pervade our society.

The myth of complete intimacy

Listening to an expert on marriage some time ago, I heard a rather alarming statement. This seminar leader told his audience, "If you are not 100 percent intimate with your spouse all of the time, it is only because you don't know how. Complete intimacy can be yours if you follow the right game plan." Quite simply, however, research and experience have shown us that this isn't true. Almost all of us can grow more intimate with our spouses, and many of the books, videos, and seminars out there will help us do just that. But complete and total intimacy, total vulnerability isn't possible on this planet. The reason is simple. Our spouses are human beings, and as human beings we all share an annoying lack of perfection. Only perfect people can love perfectly, and although I love my wife deeply and think she is one of the greatest women on earth, she too has shown signs of humanity. It didn't take her long to figure out that this Prince Charming also had some rather unwieldy imperfections, and that humanity kept us and keeps everyone from perfect intimacy.

That is elementary and rather simple. The problem is that when we read the books and listen to the tapes and then follow the directions and perfect intimacy isn't the result, we question our spouses, our marriage, and ourselves. We think that somehow we have missed the boat and that it's because of the person we are with that our marriages aren't perfect. Instead of understanding that the reason your marriage partner and my

marriage partner sometimes fail at intimacy is because of who we are—
that is, sinful, fallen human beings who live in a fallen world.

Does that mean we don't work on developing intimacy and building
closeness with our spouse? Absolutely not! It does mean that we relin-
quish the idea that this person will completely and forever meet our need
for intimacy.

The myth of the mystical spark

One woman walking away from a decent ten-year marriage told me
that it was because she no longer felt a "mystical spark" with her husband. Without that spark, she reasoned, marriage was pointless. Her
words may have been a bit overblown, but what she was referring to was
what we used to call, rather ambiguously, "chemistry." Over the years
chemistry has been expanded into something that encompasses the spiritual connectedness and the sexual attraction that men and women feel
toward each other. The myth is that it stays forever, and that if it goes
away, the marriage is over. Let me be frank. You may feel chemistry with
other people throughout your life; after a certain number of years it may
not be with your husband or wife. The reason, of course, is that mystical
sparks tend to fade away with familiarity, and that after sleeping with the
same person for fifteen years it is very difficult to be surprised. If you
want to base your marriage on chemistry, be prepared for a life filled with
different romantic partners, because it will take someone new to entice
you, to produce that chill, that sensational thrill. It may last three months
or three years, but chasing the mystical spark will lead you from person
to person.

The myth of the perfect match

Will and Tracy were beginning to wonder whether they were "wrong for each other." They were concerned that their needs and desires no longer matched, and maybe they would be better off with other people. The truth is that none of us can completely meet every need of another person. We will always fail them in some way; we will always fall short.

We live in a selfish society that urges each of us to pursue our own desires. We are told from a very young age that having our needs met is the most important thing in the world. Our expectation for our marriage partner is that he or she will meet our needs, even as those needs change and evolve, and all too often we walk away when some need goes unmet. I don't think we can say this strongly enough—no one on this earth can meet all of your needs. No one! There isn't the perfect match; at some point you will fail each other.

There Is Hope!

At this point you may be reeling. We've just told you not to expect complete intimacy, that the spark that drove you to marriage may go away, and that at some point you'll have to settle for less than you need. It isn't a pretty picture. But don't stop reading here. There is hope, and it lies not in pat answers or a "Pollyanna" approach expecting that if we just believe hard enough, things will get better. Our hope lies in understanding our limitations, reducing our expectations, and learning to nurture our marriages into what they can become.

Although we can never experience complete and utter intimacy, in fact, it is in marriage that we have the opportunity to build the most intimate relationship of our lives. Understanding that it will never be "enough" takes the pressure off of our relationship and allows us to enjoy each other and to build the friendship from which intimacy grows. We aren't telling you to give up on intimacy. We are telling you to give up the idea that you will always be at a high level of intimacy and that your marriage is in trouble if you aren't.

Marriage can be about chemistry, but sometimes you have to create it. Sometimes you have to wait for it to come back, and sometimes you have to live without it. There are scores of good books written on putting the romance back into your marriage. Our point is that you understand that just because the romance is gone doesn't mean you are in the wrong marriage. That mystical spark may flicker on and off your entire life. Enjoy it when it's there with your spouse, but know that it is a transitory thing and will come and go.

A New Image

Unfortunately, Judy's romantic ideals were dashed not long after we said, "I do." I turned out to be remarkably difficult to live with, and she showed a few human flaws as well. Our ideals were gone. So what did we have left? We had to create a new image of marriage, one that is based on reality and a hard-won love that withstands the vagaries of emotion and chemistry. Some friends described this new image for me when they talked about their life together.

"I know he's not perfect, and I know that we aren't the exciting couple we used to be. But we are something more now. We are a family. We raise our children; we live our lives together. On purpose we have chosen to be together, and although sometimes I want more, I remind myself every day of his kindness and his soft humor. Do I long for the big,

Romeo and Juliet love? Sometimes, but then I remember where they ended up. And then I realize that watching TV together twice a week, well, it isn't the greatest, but it is us, together, and that's pretty good."

I think they're right, and even more I believe that God's ideals for marriage are very different from ours. And, after all, it is His ideals and His expectations that really matter. We'll say more about this later, but right now, let it be said that God's ideals aren't about romance and chemistry. They have to do with things like commitment, trust, respect, honesty, and, most of all, a deep, abiding, and thoughtful choice to love.

In the next chapters we're going to examine how our culture, our families, and our insecurities and needs contribute to unrealistic expectations of marriage. We're going to examine the reasons we feel trapped, bored, and even sometimes angry. But we're not going to stop there. We are going to close the book by helping you choose to make your marriage the best it can be. We believe you can do it, we believe you can make it, and we believe God will help.

Romantic Ideal Checklist

Instructions: Read each statement carefully and honestly. Check (✓) the statements which you believe are true of you. Share your answers with your partner. Discuss the implications of your answers. How might your ideals and expectations be affecting your marriage relationship?

__ I am a bit idealistic when it comes to romance.

__ My expectation for intimacy is somewhat unrealistic.

__ I often find myself looking and longing for that "mystical spark" in our relationship.

__ Sometimes I am disappointed that we are not the "perfect match."

__ I am quite realistic about romance. The romantic ideal is not my goal.

__ Most of the time I am happy with the degree of intimacy in our marriage.

__ We are growing together with the years of marriage.

__ I have a realistic view of our relationship.

__ Progress in our relationship is more important than the "perfect match."

CHAPTER 2

What Cinderella Really Wanted... Our Hunger for Love and Affection

L ooking back, Cinderella had to admit that her family had been more than a little dysfunctional. Often, when the prince was off hunting wild boars and she was alone in the castle with the kids and that perennially leaky roof in the throne room, she would wonder why she had jumped into this marriage at all. It had something to do with her family. At least that was what the royal marriage therapist had told her. He had encouraged her to look back over her life, to try to determine

why she had impulsively married the prince. And looking back, well, it didn't take a wizard to figure out that she had lacked a little in the love and affection department.

Her story was familiar, even to her. Her father had been a good man, but being a product of the Middle Ages, expressing love had been difficult for him. Even when Cinderella's mother passed away, he only briefly held young Cinderella, and then soon, too soon for his daughter, her father had married again. And not long after that, he had passed away as well, a victim of yet another plague making its way through the kingdom. Cinderella's stepmother had been civil while her father was alive, but following his death, she was positively hateful. Looking back, Cinderella shuddered at the memory. For seven long years she had served as a slave in her own home, while her ugly and obnoxious stepsisters constantly made fun of her. Meanwhile, her stepmother constantly tormented her. Cinderella had no one to love, and no one loved her. After a while, she began to doubt that she was lovable.

Was it any wonder she asked herself if she had prematurely jumped into a marriage with the first man who treated her with kindness? Her therapist would have some good advice for her on this one. Summoning her maids, she gathered her things for yet another session with him, wondering all the time what was taking the prince so long to return from the hunt.

Our Hidden Hungers

We met, we fell in love, and we got married. That is usually the litany I get when couples come to me for counseling and I ask them why they got married. "We got married because we were in love." I smile, pause, and sometimes ask, "What did love mean to you then, and what does it mean to you now?" It's a difficult and unfair question because love defies explanation, is often irrational, and seems to keep changing. But the point behind the question is a fair one: What was it about this other person that made you want to be with him or her? Or even more to the point: What did this other person do for you that made you want to be with him or her? Or even: What is it about you that caused you to want to be with this person? These are hard questions to answer, but asking them honestly and working out the answers helps us discover the whys about our marriage. And if we understand what it was we were looking for when we said I do, we will understand how to avoid saying, "I don't love him or her anymore."

Jan and Robert are not your ordinary couple. Robert is wealthy and the scion of an old Southern family. Jan is a working-class girl, who happened to meet Robert at a gas station. They fell in love, they got married, and now, nine years later, they are in trouble. Robert feels increasingly claustrophobic in his marriage. He still believes he loves Jan, but he says she is driving him crazy. Jan's response is to try to hold on to him even tighter. She often puts him in positions where he has to choose between her wishes and doing something with his friends or his own family. In their marriage there are a lot of ultimatums, and if Robert doesn't respond in the "right" way, there are tears and angry recriminations.

Jan and Robert have different needs. Jan's overriding need is for love and affection, while Robert grew up in a close but unaffectionate family. He isn't comfortable with public kisses or even holding hands. Frankly, it embarrasses him. Jan craves that kind of attention, especially in front of Robert's family. She has never felt as though she belongs in his world, and when he is cold to her in public, she dies a little inside. Lying not so far beneath the surface, she is always asking the question: Does he love me? Is he going to leave?

Our needs for love and affection often drive us into marriage. And that is not necessarily a bad thing because certainly we can begin to have those needs met in a loving and committed marital relationship. The problems occur in two ways. Number one, when we realize that our needs for love and affection far outweigh our partner's ability to meet them; and number two, when we begin to think that in our rush to have those needs met, we have made a mistake in choosing our life partner.

Why Did I Do This?

I talk to many men and women who are asking the same questions Cinderella asked at the beginning of this chapter. Why did I fall in love with this guy or this girl? Did I just respond to some need, or was it something more than that? At the risk of sounding like Cinderella's therapist, I think it is instructive to look at our own backgrounds as we attempt to answer this question. For Judy and me the answers were found in her early life experiences, notably the death of her father.

It was a cold February day. I had worn my snowsuit to kindergarten, and I was going to see my dad in the hospital after school. There was knock on the classroom door, and my teacher stepped into the hallway. Half a minute later she was back. Tears were in her eyes as she walked to my desk. "Judy, your aunt and uncle are here to take you home early." I gathered up my things, climbed into the back of my uncle's car, and listened to him tell me that my father had died of a heart attack. I was five, my sister was three, and my brothers were twelve and eighteen. At forty-three, my dad was gone; at forty-three, my mother was alone. My life in its relative comfort and ease would never be the same.

My father was a successful businessman, but he hadn't planned on leaving us so soon. We were quickly in very reduced circumstances. I wore hand-me-down clothes; my mother told me how poor we were, how we didn't measure up to the rest of the family, and how everyone was better than us. I believed her. She worked hard to keep the family together, but it drained her of her optimism and her vitality, and all I knew was an exhausted woman who loved me dearly, but couldn't even begin to meet my needs.

I guess it was inevitable that a fatherless girl would fall in love with a man four years her senior. It was inevitable that he would be a strong man who took charge. It was almost guaranteed that when I found someone who told me I was beautiful and held me close that I would give everything to be with that person. I was starved for affection and dying for love, and Jerry made me feel as though I was safe—and that I was somebody. So I married him. I loved him you see...

Judy's feelings are instructive, because many of us marry out of a need for love and affection. Often we missed our father's touch or lacked his approval. Or perhaps Mom was just too busy, and we felt that she didn't care. Maybe we just walked around our entire lives feeling unlovable, and when someone finally did love us, well, we couldn't tie that person down fast enough. There are some things we need to realize as we look at our lives, some hard truths we need to understand.

Too many of us walk into marriage because of our needs for love and affection; too many of us walk back out later when those needs go unmet. The simple truth is that some of us have an insatiable need for love and affection, and no mere human can ever meet that need. The hole in our souls is too big for any one person to fill. But rather than face that unpleasant truth we choose to believe that we have married the wrong person or the person we have married is not providing enough love for us. We fail to see that it is our unmeetable need that lies at the center of our problems.

Frank is a successful businessman. He works long hours for a large company, and his labors have been rewarded. He drives a new Mercedes, lives in a new house, and his wife's clothes have all the right labels. On Saturday evenings Frank is often with his girlfriend, but he is sure to be in church every Sunday morning. When we met Frank, his double life was tearing him apart, but he was unable to really deal with his emotions. He kept talking about how his wife was cold, how she didn't really love him, and how this other person was the only person who really under-stood him. His wife was mystified and hurt. She told us that she had done her best to be the kind of caring and loving wife Frank had always want-ed. But she had a life too, and the kids needed her, and she couldn't be there for Frank every single minute. Frank's deeply felt insecurities put him in a position where an affair was easy. It met his need for love and acceptance, even as it tore at his soul and threatened to destroy all that he had worked for.

Frank believed that his wife was the problem, but over time he began to see that it was his unrealistic expectations, brought on by his need for constant love and affection, that were at the root of his problem. This need led him to a place where sin was easy, and doing the right thing very difficult.

Frank wanted out of his marriage. He believed the affair was his only chance for true happiness and having his needs met, something he felt his wife could not do. When we talked with Frank, we concentrated on three areas. We talked about understanding his past, the stages of love, and the development of realistic expectations for love, sex, and affection. All of us who wish to avoid Frank's trap and dilemma, not to mention the pain and hurt he is both dealing with and inflicting on his wife, would do well to pay attention to these three areas.

Frank and Judy have much in common. Both needed to understand the past. Judy grew up without a father telling her she was terrific. She never had a dad who hugged her after the boys teased her, never had the reassuring father's touch on her arm when life got tough. It isn't much of a stretch and certainly doesn't take a rocket scientist to draw a correlation between the absence of a father in Judy's life and her hunger for love and affection.

In our work for our book on fathers and daughters we found that women who had good relationships with their dads married later and were more likely to stay married. They reported less of a hunger for love and affection. They didn't rush into relationships that met their immediate needs; they waited and were more likely to marry mature men with the qualities necessary to make a successful marriage.

What does this mean for you as a woman? If you're struggling in your marriage or are looking to get married, you need to come to grips with your relationship with your father. Whether your relationship was good, bad, or indifferent, you need to be honest and spend some time reflecting on how that relationship has met or influenced your needs and your hopes for marriage. One daughter, ending a ten-year marriage, put it this way: "I guess I married to find a dad, and the funny thing is, I found one, just like my dad. Never there, never caring about me, just selfish and looking out for himself."

We take all of our past experiences into our marriages. Some of those experiences have brought us great joy. But we also take our pain, our hurts, and our disappointments into marriage. We hope that our husband or our wife will be able to help fill the emptiness in our souls. Women who never felt approval from their dads look to their husbands for the kind of support and love that only a father can give. And often when the husband falls short in giving that love and support, these women are disappointed and disillusioned, and they want out.

Pay attention to your past. Listen to your life. What has gone before makes a big difference in what will come next—not because of some psychological theory or because Oprah says so. We are, at least in part, the sum total of our experiences. The events in our lives have shaped us, and to deny that is to deny reality. And when it comes to women, the research is clear: Nothing shapes women like their relationships with their fathers.

What should you be looking for? When assessing your past, look at three different areas. First of all, was your father there? Was he a part of your life? Was he a fixture, someone you could count on? A father's presence does a great deal to calm the insecurities of his daughters; a father's absence feeds these insecurities, insecurities that only grow with age.

Second, was your father affirming? When researching *Fathers and Daughters*, we were awestruck by the power of a father's words to his daughter. Fathers who spread praise around generously were more likely to have confident daughters who were not starved for love and affection.

Fathers who found 100 different ways to say "very good" had daughters who grew up knowing they mattered and had value. If your dad was that kind of dad, thank God for him every night, because he truly was a gift.

On the other hand, if all you knew was the back of his hand or the curl of his lip after yet another sarcastic remark, you carry an entirely more burdensome load into your marriage. If all you heard was how stupid, ugly, and useless you were, your road will be more difficult.

The third thing to look for is friendship with your dad. Has he bestowed the gift of friendship on you now that you are an adult? Does he treat you like an equal, asking your opinion and listening when you speak? Dads who give the gift of friendship to their daughters tell their daughters how valuable and terrific they are, and treat them with respect as an adult. Dads who fail to give their daughters that gift may end up with daughters who are constantly seeking that final stage of approval, looking for it in the men they date and marry.

It is not just women who need to look into their past for keys to their future. Men need to look honestly at their own families. And men also need to look long and hard at their dads, asking some of the same questions their wives need to ask. As men we learn about manhood from our own fathers as we watch our dads interact with our moms and others. We learn how men treat women and what marriage is supposed to be.

We also come out of our families with unique experiences that shape who we are. One young man put it to me rather poignantly after a long counseling session: "Jerry, you are the first man who has ever listened to me. I know that for me marriage was an attempt to find someone whom I could talk to and who would listen. I remember my dad, and he was always too busy to talk. He never seemed to care." This young man went on, rather bitterly, "Dad never even tried to give us what we needed. I don't ever remember a kiss or even a gentle gesture of any kind. I'm sure my incredible need to touch my wife and have her hold me and tell me often how much she loves me got its start right there."

I think he was probably right, but understanding your past is only the first step, although it is a huge one. We need to understand our past not to blame our shortcomings and failures on our parents. We understand our past to learn from it and to take the steps necessary to grow into the kind of people God wants us to be.

We cannot stop with just understanding. We need to move into growth, dealing with the issues from our past and moving beyond them into a mature, adult view of life. Adults don't run from their past. They embrace the good things that God brought to them through their parents, and healthy adults learn from the rest. It isn't about someone to blame; it's about a way to learn.

The Stages of Love

We all know that romance doesn't last forever; at least we claim to know that. Why then do we desert our marriages when the romance dies? Why do some of us spend our lives looking for that undying mystical spark? It may be that we don't understand the different stages of love. Psychologist Patricia Love in her book *Hot Monogamy* lists three stages: attraction, infatuation, and attachment.

Research tells us that relationships move in a fairly predictable arc. The initial stage is attraction. We know what that feels like. Remember the girl in the eighth grade, when she looked right at you and the hair on your arms stood on end? Or when that boy walked into the room and your stomach did a flip-flop. That is attraction. As we grow older our hair sometimes still stands on end, but we are attracted in other ways that are not just sexual. We feel drawn to people because we share affinities with them. We like someone's sense of humor, his laugh, his smile, or his mind. We read the same things and listen to the same music. We are attracted to them. And in that initial attraction there is possibility, and the possibilities add to the attraction. As we get to know the person, we may move from attraction to full-blown infatuation. This is what most of us call love, and few of us make it out of this stage before we get married. When we are infatuated, we are looking for the good in the other person, refusing to see the negative. We are spending an enormous amount of time together, learning about each other. It is fun; it is often very sensual, and we don't think this feeling will ever end. So we decide to get married, because we've never felt this way about anyone before. It won't go away, because it is too real, too exciting, and too vibrant. How could this kind of love ever stop? The world is sunny and bright; the food tastes better when we are with this person. Movies are funnier and sunsets more beautiful, all because we are "in love." It won't ever change, we think; it won't ever go away; it's too intense to ever fade.

Researchers tell us that infatuation does go away. In fact, as early as three months into the marriage, and usually lasting no later than eighteen months. Harville Hendricks and Helen Hunt say it very well in their great book, *The Couple's Companion*: "Romantic love is nature's anesthesia, a dirty trick to bond us to our partner so that we are willing to go through the struggle to real love" (1994, p. 278).

After infatuation we must choose attachment, the third stage of love. Many of us never do that. We keep trying to rekindle the early infatuation. Sometimes we do that through elaborate sexual games; sometimes through something as simple as revisiting the scene of past passion. Some of us attend various seminars hoping that the passion will return and the spark will catch fire. Much of what passes for marriage renewal is our attempt to rekindle infatuation. It may work for a short time, but usually does not last. In the end it takes more to achieve less until it feels like there is nothing left. The answer is not re-infatuation, but progressing to commitment and attachment. But we shy away from attachment because of the plain old vanilla commitment required to build true love.

We don't want to be attached to someone; we don't really want commitment; we want to be infatuated, because nothing in the world feels as great as infatuation. Sometimes we blame the other person for our lack of infatuation; sometimes we blame ourselves. The one thing we believe is that our relationship isn't working, and it's time to get out! When we are hungering for love and affection, infatuation meets our needs, but when it begins to fade, our insatiable needs rise to the surface again. Our lover and partner is no longer able to meet those needs, and we are disappointed.

It doesn't have to be that way. We can choose to live a committed life, moving beyond endless attempts to revive infatuation or to find it with another person. But it takes work and sacrifice, and most of all we have to recognize that our needs for love and affection may be partially unmet, and that's OK.

Develop Realistic Expectations for Love, Sex, and Affection

One sure-fire way to help your marriage is to develop realistic marriage expectations. One study of fifty couples interviewed about their marital expectations six months before and six months after their weddings showed that two of their strongest expectations were affection (women) and sex (men). Six months after their wedding the two biggest disappointments were affection (women) and sex (men). What we want and hope for the most from our marriages has the potential to cause us the greatest disappointment. Recently I talked with a thirty-four-year-old woman, who was struggling with her feelings toward her husband of seven years. In her words, "I think I like him, but as far as love, it's at zero right now, nothing, zip." She went on to describe how he had held her before they were married and how she had felt safe in his arms. He had treated her so differently than her abusive father and the string of abusive boyfriends. But now when he reached for her, it always was a precursor to or an argument about sex. She said, "I don't want him touching me sexually. Not at all. Doesn't he understand that I just want be held—I mean without having to pay a sexual toll."

Take a deep breath here and let it out slowly, because what we are about to say isn't easy to hear, and you may be tempted to blow it off, to read it and not take it to heart. No one will ever satisfy all of your needs. No one. Guys, no woman will ever completely satisfy your sexual desire. No one.

Listening to the radio not long ago, I heard an old rock song from the late seventies. The band Journey was singing about a woman who said, "Anyway you want it, that's the way you need it, any way you want it...." The song goes on in rather indelicate detail, "She said, 'All night, oh all night, oh every night.'" A passenger in the car said, "Hey, that's the kind of girl I'm looking for." The voice from a married, worldly wise female passenger in the backseat advised solemnly, "Don't waste your time. She doesn't exist." Yet we do look for the woman who will satisfy our every need. Because Journey sang about her, she must be real. And women believe that somewhere out there the completely sensitive guy exists; you've seen him in the movies; you've read about him in the novels; surely he is just around the corner. But he's not. And she's not. They're not. And if you and I spend our time and energy trying to find the person who will meet our unrealistic needs for sex, love, and affection, we are going to live very disappointing lives.

Cinderella stamped her foot impatiently. She didn't like what the royal marriage therapist was telling her. He was making her sound romantically foolish, surely her expectations weren't out of line. All she wanted was unconditional love and acceptance. Why couldn't the prince give her that? The therapist was talking. "Princess, you need to redefine what you mean by love. You need to develop realistic expectations, and you need to be proactive in building a strong love for the prince."

"Humph," she stamped again. "My fairy godmother could just as well have left me with my stepmother. In so many ways I'm just as lonely as I was then. As a matter of fact I'm the same person I was back then when I was miserable. Why, I thought marrying the prince would change all that!"

The therapist smiled. He hadn't become the royal marriage therapist by accident, and he was wise and had seen many a prince and princess falter on the road to love. "My princess, you are exactly the same person you were before. You are what you have experienced, and you can no more escape that than a zebra can change its stripes. So learn from it, and grow from what you know."

"But I need him to hold me. I need to know he still cares,

and I need some romance, some tingle in my bones when he looks at me. I need to feel like I did when he put the glass slipper on my foot. What am I to do?"

All of us need to learn four simple things as we try to deal with our hunger for love, sex, and affection. Your partner will not meet all of your needs. You will need to redefine love continually, seeking to move from infatuation to attachment. Sex is not the end-all, be-all. It is an important expression of intimacy, but in the scale of things it shouldn't make or break your marriage. Love is active, not passive. Erich Fromm puts it brilliantly in his classic work, *The Art of Loving*: "Love is an activity, not a passive affect. It is a standing in, not a falling for. In the most general way the active character of love can be described by stating that love is primarily giving, not receiving. Love is the active concern for the life and growth of that which we love." Of course, that idea isn't original with Fromm. He is merely echoing the words of the Apostle Paul, written nearly 2,000 years earlier: "Love is patient, love is kind. It does not envy, it does not boast, it is not proud. It is not rude, it is not self-seeking, it is not easily angered, it keeps no record of wrongs. . . . It always protects, always trusts, always hopes, always perseveres" (1 Cor. 13:4-5, 7).

My Hidden Hungers Checklist

Instructions: Some of the following statements are more applicable to women than to men. Check (√) only those statements that are true of you. Think about and discuss with your partner the implications of your responses, and the effect of your hidden hungers on your marriage relationship.

___ My father was always there for me while I was growing up.

___ My father often used positive words of affirmation with me.

___ My father's friendship meant a lot to me.

___ I have always longed for my father's presence in my life.

___ All my life I have desired my father's approval.

___ I have always felt the need to feel attractive to men.

___ I seem to have a hunger for love that is not easily satisfied.

___ My idea of love seems to fit the definition of infatuation.

___ My expectations for love and affection are more idealistic than realistic.

CHAPTER 3

Why Prince Charming Is Always Riding in the Woods: Our Need to Rescue Others

he boar had eluded him again. Sometimes being a prince was a tough job. He didn't even really like hunting wild boars, but as his father had said so many times, "It's what the people want; you've got to give the people what they want." So wild boar hunting it was. Still he missed Cinderella and wondered how she was doing. Reflecting on her, he realized that she had been a little cut of sorts around the palace lately. Sort of morose and moody. Come to think of it, he had been a little disappointed in her as well. The spark seemed to have gone out of their life together. Sex certainly wasn't what it once was. With a rueful grin the Prince remembered their whirlwind courtship and how he had seen her at the ball. She was so beautiful, so spectacularly unlike any of the other girls he had danced with that night. She glowed with effervescence, but there was tragedy in her eyes as well. Then with the stroke of twelve she was gone, and he was left with nothing but a beautiful, petite glass slipper. He had scoured the kingdom looking for her, and then on that magical day he found her. The slipper fit, and he took her away from her life of pain. He felt good at that thought, because he really had been princely about that aspect of his life at least. He had rescued a damsel in distress. Remembering her hateful stepmother, the prince shuddered at the thought. And those disgusting stepsisters, they were truly unattractive people. He had literally ridden in on his white horse and taken her away from all that drudgery and her servant-like existence. She had been so grateful at first, but now, well, it was hard to keep saving someone. She was out of danger; the rescue was over; and happily ever after was a whole lot more boring than he had ever dreamed.

A cry interrupted his reverie. It was a woman's voice, coming from a dark thicket to his left, and she was in need. His pulse quickened as he turned his horse toward the sound.

Lori was thirty-six, divorced, raising three children. And she was lonely. At the suggestion of a friend she joined a Christian singles group. She met a man who seemed to be the answer to her prayers. He listened to her and cared about her. He talked openly about his faith. Sure he had some problems. He had been bankrupt, and he told her about a business deal gone sour. She loaned him money to help him out. Soon they were sleeping together, and then he moved in. She didn't mind working while he stayed home and helped with the kids, but then she began to notice some disturbing tendencies. He would go out with some friends after she came home from work, and he would return drunk. But he was struggling; he needed her help; and honestly, it felt good to have someone to hold, someone who needed her and told her so. When she finally walked down the aisle with him, her friends were openly skeptical. They thought Tony was using her, and they didn't see what she was getting out of the deal, but as she carefully explained to me in my office, she liked helping Tony, and soon he would be back on his feet. It really wasn't a problem. I asked her, "If it really wasn't a problem, why did you come in to see me?" She replied, "We seem to be drifting apart lately. What can I do to grow closer to Tony?" He was gone so much now, and she was worried that she was going to lose him. They had been married three years.

William worked for Tricia's dad, and she met him at work. He was older, more experienced, and had an aura of danger about him. He drove a big Harley-Davidson motorcycle and had a big hearty laugh. He was always smiling a secret smile, like the rest of the world didn't get the joke. He entranced Tricia. Nevertheless, her dad caught him stealing from the business and fired him. She moved in with him two weeks later. When the police busted him for possession of drugs, everyone told her he was hopeless and she should give up on him. But she knew there was a good man inside of William; he just needed a good woman to help him stay on the straight and narrow. Tricia saw him as a challenge and paid for his stint in a rehab clinic. Two months later he was back in jail, but it didn't matter, she wasn't going to give up on him as everyone else had. She would save him. Tricia's parents related her story to me with tearful pauses and angry glances. They didn't know how to help their daughter, but they were sure she was being led down the wrong path. They had been driven to calling for help because Tricia had announced that she was going to marry William, and they couldn't stop her.

Gary was a widower trying to raise three boys. He was also a teacher in the Christian school where Mary worked. She admired him. He was fifteen years her senior and seemed so wise and thoughtful. She had never married but soon began to think about a life with him. They became friends, then they became more than friends. She started helping him with his kids, saw the value she could bring to his lonely life, and said yes before he finished asking. She was going to rescue those motherless children and shelter this caring, lonely man. Reality set in two years later. He was busy; the kids were demanding and not particularly accepting of their new mom. And the instant family had been tough on her as well, she now confided to Judy. It seemed as though she was the one in need of rescuing. Only there was no way out.

The role of the rescuing prince or princess can be irresistible. Who can forget the sweet prince of our childhood fairy tales arriving in the nick of time to rescue the princess. Who can forget the Brady Bunch and the mutual rescuing that this stepfamily seemed to have down pat? And wasn't Florence Henderson a wonderful mother to those three boys? And where would Marcia, Jan, and Cindy be without their stepdad? It is a role we see ourselves in all too often. Many of us walk down the aisle because we are in love, but some of us are in love with rescuing others. Sometimes the opportunity to be the heroine or the hero is too golden to pass up. Sometimes the other person is too needy to leave in the gutter. Sometimes our need to help is irresistible, and we swoop in for the rescue. Some would say, "That's OK." Tricia and Lori would tell you a different story, as would Judy's friend. Marriages that start off as rescue missions often end aborted in court.

Why does this happen and what drives us to rescue others? In this chapter we'll take a look at those questions. The answers may be hard for some of us to take, but honesty will show us a way to build marriages that will last for many years after the dragon has been slain and the princess rescued from her peril.

The Right Thing for the Wrong Reason

Helping others is a good thing. Lending a listening ear to a friend in need; loaning a struggling parent a few dollars; believing in someone whom others have given up on. These are all good things. Done for the right reasons they are the attributes of a healthy caring person. But many of us help others not because we feel compelled by the morality of helping the downtrodden. We rescue because it feeds our own needs. We need to feel valuable and important, and when we rescue others, we feel that way. Pat Springle (*Co-Dependency*, p. 50) describes this well: "If someone has a need, I'll meet it! If there's not a need, I'll find one, and then I'll meet it! If there's a small need, I'll make it a large one. Then I'll feel even better when I meet it! Even if nobody wants help, I'll help anyway! Then when I've helped, I'll feel good about myself!"

When someone in our life needs us desperately, maybe couldn't even live without us, we feel as though we have purpose and meaning. It is very easy to confuse altruism and selfishness. If we are helping others to meet our own needs, we are doing the right thing for the wrong reason. And when you marry someone to rescue him or her, you are doing the wrong thing for the right reasons. Let me explain. When we marry someone to rescue that person from poverty, drugs, a bad home life, their own bad habits, or poor choices, we need for them to continue to be sick and needy. If they get better, then we are no longer vital to their survival. If they get well, the foundation of the relationship ceases to exist. Our interest in that person, and often that person's interest in us, will wane quickly. This situation can get ugly when in our attempt to rescue another person, we sabotage the rescue because we desire them to stay needy. Psychologists call this co-dependency, and it is a treacherous foundation for a marriage.

Springle lists three primary characteristics of co-dependency: (1) A lack of objectivity; (2) A warped sense of responsibility; and (3) Being easily controlled and controlling others. He defines co-dependency as "a compulsion to control and rescue others by fixing their problems." This is a great definition but not a great attribute to possess. We end up feeding off each other's sicknesses, and the result is two people who are worse off in a downward spiraling relationship.

How does this happen? The answer isn't that simple, and the roots of the problem are often tangled and difficult to discern. But at a basic level all of us need to feel valuable, and we need to have purpose in life. Some of us have built a healthy identity that is secure and strong. Our value and purpose comes from realizing that God loves us and has gifted each of us uniquely. But many of us, for different reasons, haven't come to that level of mental health. And some of us see ourselves as valuable only when we are helping others. We fail to realize our own intrinsic worth, and instead, we seek to find value in the eyes of others. So we continue to rescue needy and sick people. More than occasionally we call that feeling of euphoria we have when we feel needed and wanted "love," and marriage is the result. Sadly, however, trouble is just around the corner.

Our Partner's Needs Are Greater Than Our Ability to Meet Them

Three things happen when we marry to rescue others. Number one, we find that some people are the human equivalent of black holes. Black holes are pockets in space where gravity is so strong that even light cannot escape. That perfectly describes some of the people we try to rescue.

These people have long-standing problems that they really do not want to fix, and despite our best efforts, their needs are just too great. We will never fill their need; it is a black hole into which we can pour our love and concern, as well as the best years of our lives, but in the end it amounts to nothing. The needs are just too great. Frustrated, drained, and angry, we want out of the marriage. However, we don't dare to leave because our partner would implode without us. So we toil on, giving and giving, getting more and more angry, letting the resentment build. When we can't take it anymore, we just walk away. That is Karen's story. She was married at twenty-three to Fred, a man with a genius IQ who could barely tie his shoes. Karen left after thirteen years of marriage and two children. She told her counselor, "I just couldn't take it anymore. He was like a small child—he couldn't hold a job, and he couldn't even mow the lawn. I gave and I gave, but it was never enough. He wanted more and more. I had believed that I could coax him out of his shell after we were married, but now I know that all there is to him is a shell." To paraphrase someone, there is no one there.

Karen's story is extreme but hardly unique for men and women who marry black holes. It doesn't have to end that way. If you are married to a black hole, we encourage you to keep on reading. Although your disappointment and disillusion may be driving you out of your marriage, in the last third of this book you will find hope and healing, as well as a way to cope with a person whose needs are so great.

We Do Not Like the Person We Are Becoming

After twenty years of marriage Andy had been through enough and moved out. His wife was impossible, and he refused to put up with her any longer. He had tried to help her through her periodic bouts with depression. He had gone to hundreds of hours of therapy with her. He had helped when she was on her medication and stuck with her when she was off her medication. He had paid for acupuncture and a trip to a Maharishi who promised her enlightenment. But no more! What had once brought pleasure to him—helping his emotionally delicate wife—now only brought pain. He didn't like the person he had become. He had turned into a nag, where once he had been a concerned nurse.

When I saw Andy, he was out of the house and had both feet firmly planted outside of the marriage. Meeting her needs no longer brought him a feeling of purpose; it just wore him out. The reason for the relationship had ceased. By his standards, the marriage had no future.

We Find Ourselves in Need of Rescue

When our partner's needs become overwhelming and his or her struggles draw us inexorably in, we find that the rescuer is in need of rescue. When Jamie was eighteen, she took off with her father's car and her boyfriend. A rival gang had marked him for murder, and she had "borrowed" the car to get him safely out of town. Once they hit Las Vegas, they decided to get married. When they hit San Diego, she was broke, afraid, and ready to come home. In fact, her rescue had become an adventure of a different sort, and now she was in need of help.

Marriages that begin with a rescue attempt often end up in divorce court because it seems as though divorce court is the only place the rescuer can find relief. The other person's problems have become overwhelming and often scary. The needs have grown too great; the addictions are threatening the children; the repo-man is at the door for the car; and the only way out, the only way to find any rescue ourselves, is by bailing out of the marriage.

A Better Way... Hope, Health, and Discovery

There is hope for the rescuer, the fixer, and the co-dependent spouse. And it's not necessary to get out of the marriage to fix yourself. That's right, you need to fix yourself, not the other person. The first thing for the fixer to do is to recognize that this behavior is not healthy, either for the rescuer or the rescued. Continued rescuing only perpetuates the other person's problems and continues to make that person dependent on you, the rescuer. Of course, some of us like that; that's why we keep doing it. However, that locks the other person (and us) into a lifetime of dependency and uncertainty. God's plan for us is to "build each other up," not make others dependent upon us, even if it does feel good.

Not only is this behavior unhealthy for the person being constantly rescued, but it is also unhealthy for the rescuer. The rescuer tends to find much of his or her identity in the other person, instead of developing a separate identity. Developmental psychologists call this process individuation, or simply, becoming a unique individual. This process ought to occur; if it does not, the dysfunction has become a lifelong pattern.

Once you stop and recognize your need to fix or rescue as unhealthy, you can move on to the second step—getting to know the special person God designed you to be . . . one of a kind. That's not weird; it's unique, and it's OK. You actually have the right to be you. In fact, God desires it, for He made you very special. Indeed, the psalmist said, "For you created my inmost being; you knit me together in my mother's womb" (Ps. 139:13). The writer did not get angry with God for making him special, nor was he disgusted with the person he had become. His response was "I praise you because I am fearfully and wonderfully made; your works are wonderful, I know that full well. My frame was not hidden from you when I was made in the secret place. When I was woven together in the depths of the earth, your eyes saw my unformed body. All the days ordained for me were written in your book before one of them came to be" (vv. 14-16).

God has made each of us special beings, not only to *be* special, but also to *do* special things, which He has planned for us to do. It is only by discovering the real person we are that we can accomplish the real plan for which God has made us. If our identity is found in another person, that wonderful plan will never be realized. Start now to look at yourself objectively. Don't be afraid of what you might see. Ask others what they like about you. Write down what you like about yourself. Allow yourself to think good thoughts about yourself. What are your positive attributes? What are your negative attributes? Write them down. They too are part of you. Learn to live with them, but do not focus on them, or be overwhelmed by them. Begin to discover yourself, daily. Allow yourself to be surprised by yourself. Begin to appreciate the person whom God has designed. Don't depend on someone else to make you whole. God is perfectly willing to continue His work in you while conforming you into the image of His Son, Jesus. As you become more and more like Him, you will realize the wonderful truth about being a Christian, a Christ-one. That's true identity for the believer.

Need to Rescue Checklist

Instructions: Carefully read the following questions. Check (√) each statement that is true of you. If your responses indicate that you are a rescuer, share that with a pastor or counselor, especially if that need is negatively impacting your life and marriage.

___ I often find myself rescuing others from difficult situations.

___ I get a lot of satisfaction when I am rescuing someone.

___ I am sometimes frustrated when others resist my rescue attempts.

___ I sometimes find the needs of others too difficult for me to meet.

___ I wonder if my need to help others is really a need to help myself.

___ My whole life seems to be wrapped up in others and their needs.

___ I seldom find time for me and my needs.

___ I feel guilty when I look out for myself.

___ When I am really honest with myself, I realize I'm tired of helping others, but this is hard for me to admit. I really shouldn't be saying this to anyone.

___ I am usually available to help someone in need.

CHAPTER 4

Our Need to Escape

"OK," thought Cinderella, "I can do this." She steeled herself and began to think back over the years before the prince had swept her away. Her therapist had asked her to exorcise her past and to think about her life, but it was so hard. She had tried to put all the pain and the loneliness behind her, tried to forget the indignities and the petty hurts that had wounded her so deeply and so often. Now she was supposed to bring it all back. Now it was going to be good for her to remember what had driven her to want out of her house and into the palace? "Hey, I'm not stupid," she thought for the three hundredth time; anyone would want to marry a prince. Still, trying to do as she was told and trying to put the spark back into her marriage, she would go back to those painful memories...

"Cinderella, wash the floor in my bathroom right now. I know you said you washed it yesterday, but it feels a trifle, well, sandy on my delicate feet." Drusilla, Cinderella's stepsister, was actually the kinder of the two. Rarely did she take a swat at Cinderella when telling her what to do.

Cinderella then hurried to the bathroom. In the hall she felt the sudden chill that she had come to recognize as her stepmother's presence. Coldly, her stepmother questioned, "Cinderella, whatever are you dawdling for? There is work to be done. You know I can teach you with a switch if you choose to learn the hard way." The threat was enough, Cinderella had felt the sting of the switch many times before.

The memory of that moment and so many others just like it provoked a flood of tears. Alone in her palatial (although drafty) bedroom Cinderella wept. Her life had been horrible. Had it been wrong to want out? Had it been wrong to climb so eagerly behind the prince on his white horse when he came with his promise of rescue? What other choice had she really had? She had to escape or she would have died.

They were missionaries and, to all who looked at the carefully constructed façade, a happy, caring family. But behind closed doors when the ministry for the day was over, there was shouting. Things were broken, and tears were shed. The kids hid in their rooms; Mom and Dad argued; a marriage was coming to an end.

"If you hate me so much, if you have so little respect for me, if I am such an incredibly awful person, then why did you marry me?" he screamed at his wife. "Because I wanted to get out. I had to get out. My father was awful. All I saw when I saw your face was an escape hatch. Little did I know that I was running into something even worse!"

Fred and Joanne were dealing with the same reality that was slowly dawning on Cinderella. Both marriages had been escape hatches from unhealthy situations. Not a week goes by that I don't talk to a couple where at least one of the spouses married out of a need to escape. We marry to escape dysfunctional families. We marry to escape from loneliness. We marry to escape from the consequences of our own choices. We marry because we cannot bear our burdens alone. We marry because we are bored and feel marriage will add excitement. We marry because wherever we are in life, we just want out.

Kathleen was twenty-two when she met Roger. She was struggling to pay the rent as an administrative assistant with two young children from a short-lived marriage. Roger wasn't perfect, but he was employed. He took her to nice places, and before long she was "in love with him." It didn't hurt to have someone else helping with the kids, and when he asked her to marry him, she said yes without hesitation. Five years later she realizes she doesn't really have anything in common with him and doesn't really have anything to say to him. Now she is looking to escape from her escape.

The truth of the matter is that when we marry to escape, we rush into a lifelong commitment that must outlive the short-term perspective of our desperate circumstances. When we are in trouble, when we feel desperate, when we feel like our world is caving in, and when someone offers us a hand—a way out through marriage—we are all too eager to take that person up on the offer. The problem comes after we have escaped and find ourselves in a different kind of trap.

We live in a broken and fallen world. We are products of broken and fallen families, and sometimes we are afraid and need to escape. Sometimes the brokenness and the evil of people around us create an insatiable need to get out, to run, and to be protected. And that is not always wrong. Sometimes we do need to escape.

Toni was nineteen when I met her. She was getting married and coming to me at her parents' insistence. She had been living with her boyfriend for two years. She had moved in with him after ending another relationship in which she was abused physically and emotionally. Her current boyfriend was kind and gentle. He treated her with respect, and he protected her from her vengeful abuser. Toni was a woman who had had to escape. She had needed to get out of a potentially dangerous situation, but now she was looking at marriage, and with her parents' help had begun to ask some tough questions. Most importantly she asked, "Am I marrying Tom just to escape my past?" In the time we spent together, we also asked another question: "Can I deal with my past and find safety and security without rushing into marriage?"

I believe people when they tell me they needed to escape. I have spent the last twenty-five years of my life listening to stories of men and women who had been so hurt, so stifled, and so afraid they couldn't bear it anymore and needed to get out. I believe them. I also believe that escape is a woefully inadequate foundation for a marriage. Why? Because as the immediate need for safety, security, freedom, or whatever recedes, so does the need for the marriage. When we marry to escape, we inevitably put ourselves in a position where we wake up one day, find that what drove us into this marriage is no longer the most pressing issue in our lives, and then we wonder, "What comes next?"

For a teenage girl looking for a way out of a tough home situation, marriage looks like an easy answer, but all too often it is just a trading of traps, a tough family for a tough marriage. An abusive father for an abusive husband. A profound, unshakable loneliness traded for a cold, loveless marriage that produces loneliness that equals or exceeds the loneliness she tried to escape. The hard truth is that we cannot escape from ourselves. We take ourselves wherever we go, and that means we repeat the patterns of behavior that got us into trouble in the first place.

Here is where things get tricky. As we begin to realize that we haven't solved our problems by getting married, as we begin to create the same kinds of relationships and make the same kinds of mistakes that trapped us in the first place, an overwhelming need to run away again, to escape again, seizes us. And all too often we build a pattern into our lives that is very difficult to break. When things get tough, we run away.

Jim's story isn't very different from many of our own. He had a demanding dad who never affirmed him and who never told him he was great. All Jim ever knew was the fist after failure and the drunken anger that always seemed directed his way. Jim went away to college and met a young woman who loved him and told him he was special. After his sophomore year, they were married. Although he had escaped from his father's grasp, the marriage soon exhibited signs of stress. Jim needed more than his wife could give him. He needed her by his side constantly; he needed almost constant affirmation. His insecurities drove her crazy.

Meanwhile, Jim was in a graduate class with a beautiful woman two years older than he was. One day they had coffee after class. She told him he was smart and funny and that she wished they had met when he was still single. Jim shared that feeling, and three weeks later they began an affair that was still going on when the stress drove Jim to get into his car and drive until he ran out of gas, two states and three hundred and eighty-five miles later.

When I asked him what had happened, he just said, "I needed to get away. I couldn't live with myself anymore. So I just ran."

The Escape Artist

I remember turning on the TV not long ago and watching a man in a straitjacket being chained up, handcuffed, and put in leg irons. He was then sealed into a waterproof safe, which was locked and chained. A helicopter picked up the safe and dropped it into the San Francisco bay. Eight minutes later, dripping wet, the man emerged, freed of all his restraints, grinning and bowing for the cameras. The man was a magician, an escape artist. Although I have no idea how he did it, I think his act was less impressive than the men and women who have sat in my office and described escapes even more improbable than that one. These men and women have become escape artists, and no matter how badly they have chosen and how difficult their life circumstances become, they always find a way out. There is a disturbing tendency to these people. Just as the magician has to dream up ever more dangerous and difficult escapes to keep us tuned in, so does the escape artist who seems to move into more and more difficult situations. They leave in their wake hurt and wounded people, and lives of unresolved conflict and broken relationships. And even as they continue to escape, they are trapped in a cycle because they refuse to grow personally or relationally, and because they refuse to take responsibility for their actions.

The cycle goes like this: Negative situation/Possible escape/Bad choices/Negative situation/Possible escape…

The problem with running away is that we never take the time to get any real perspective on the situation or, even more importantly, on ourselves. We do not see things for what they are; we only see a threat that causes us to run. So we move from relationship to relationship, from marriage to marriage, and the underlying issues are never resolved; they are never even wrestled with because we don't take a backward glance, fearing the truth of the past will catch us.

What to Do?

"OK, Jerry and Judy, so I married to escape and now I want out again. I understand the problem, but what can I do right now? I want out, but I also want to do the right thing." Before any rash decisions are made based on a need to escape, we need to ask ourselves some tough questions and we need to answer them with honesty.

What is really driving my need to escape?

This is a vital question. I had a woman in my office two months ago who told me if she didn't get out of her house, her abusive husband would kill her. That was a real threat that demanded immediate action and escape. Finding a safe place for this woman while she tried to work on her life was vital, and we were able to help her. But most of the time the risk is not to life and limb. Most of the time what we really risk is the demolition of our carefully constructed illusions about our lives and ourselves. This is not a sufficient reason to run away.

What does God want me to learn?

I'm a pastor who believes that God teaches us through our mistakes, our pain, and our suffering. Before we run away, we need to ask ourselves what God is trying to teach us through our current circumstances. I have a motto I often share with clients and have passed on to my own children: "Never waste a bad experience." Before you run from the pain of the moment, figure out what there is to learn in that pain and what you can take with you that may prevent the same kind of mistake in the future. Too many of us run from our pain without taking the time to grow and learn, and so we find ourselves needing to escape a strikingly similar situation a few months or years down the road.

Am I becoming an escape artist?

Look at your life for patterns. Are you doing the same thing over and over? It is helpful to have a good, knowledgeable friend or counselor help you with this. It is very difficult for us to see the destructive patterns in our own lives. What is obvious to others may be oblivious to us. Ask for help and then ask the question.

What can I do, and how can I change?

Your marriage is a noose tightening around your neck. It is getting harder and harder to breathe, and you know it isn't your fault. If you could just get out of this relationship, things would be better. True? Maybe, but it is also possible that you will find peace only through taking charge of your life and refusing to run and escape. As improbable as it seems and feels, it may just be that you and I are part of the problem and that we can become part of the solution. Before running into another relationship, before feeding your desire to escape, ask yourself what you can do right now to make your current relationship a better place. Again, this is much easier and responses are usually more honest when a good counselor or pastor can help you frame the right questions and then encourage you as you look for answers together.

Where am I going?

When we run away, prepositions become important. We usually know what we are running *from*, but do we know what we are running *to*. Little words can make a big difference in our lives. Running away blinds us without consideration for the direction we are running or without any thought that our ultimate desperation will not help us. I'm reminded of the old B-grade horror movies. As the monster closes in on its prey, the victim screams and runs blindly into the dark, inevitably running right into the monster he thought he was fleeing. Some of us live our lives like that, but we don't have to.

God Is There

After asking those questions, you may still be afraid and want to end your marriage by running away, or you may want to jump into a marriage as a means of escape because it seems to be the only viable option for you. Fear has grabbed you; panic is driving you; and you feel alone. The simple truth of Christianity, however, is that you are not alone. The God who set the stars in the heavens and who makes the rain to fall and the grass to grow cares about you. He knows you and loves you, and most of all He wants the best for you. The Apostle Paul tells us in his letter to the Corinthians, "God is faithful; he will not let you be tempted beyond what you can bear" (1 Cor. 10:13). In other words, when you feel as though you're at the end of your rope, you aren't yet. God is there under you, waiting to catch you if you fall and ready to give you the strength you need to face your fears, to deal rationally with your life, and to live up to your commitments. God won't run away from you.

Escape Artist Checklist

Instructions: Read the following questions carefully and honestly. Check (√) the statements that are true of you. If your responses lead you to to believe that you have the characteristics of an escape artist, you may want to talk with a pastor or counselor, especially if this is negatively affecting your life or marriage.

___ I seem to be developing a pattern of running away from problems.

___ I find it difficult to face painful situations.

___ When the going gets tough, I get going, elsewhere.

___ I don't usually stick around long enough to learn from problems.

___ Problems are often too awful for me to face.

___ I have never really learned how to face problems in a healthy way.

___ I find it hard to delay gratification. I want relief now.

___ My tendency is to run, rather than work through problems.

___ It's hard for me to ask God to help me face a problem and grow through it.

___ I tend to ignore problems, hoping they will go away.

"It Was the Thing to Do"

J t wasn't supposed to be this way," Cinderella thought bitterly. She had done all the right things. When the Prince showed up at the door with the glass slipper and the proposal of marriage, she had been swept off her feet. She hadn't allowed reason to cloud her judgment. She hadn't given any thought to the fact that they were very young, that she hardly knew him, and that he didn't realize the extent to which her family background had created a very needy and insecure woman. They hadn't thought at all about the disparity in their backgrounds. They had decided to live the fairy tale. She had followed her heart as every heroine must, and she had waltzed into happily ever after. But it was less happy and seemed more like eternity every day. What else could she have done? Not for the last time did she curse everyone who had ever written a fairy tale. "They don't really know what it's like. They *just write the script, and I'm supposed to read the lines, but sometimes, well, the lines they write don't square with the feelings in my heart. They truly are grim. What am I supposed to do?"*

The Scriptwriters

Hollywood isn't the only place where scripts are written and acted out. Around the world, every day, men and women are living out the scripts that others have written for them. Every day men and women are getting married because it is the next thing on the list to check off; it is what their family or friends expect of them; it is the script that has been written for them. And saying no or breaking away from the screenwriter's ideal is almost impossible.

Samantha was sixteen when she met Tom. He was handsome, moody, and more than a little mysterious. They started to date, and before long she had turned her entire life over to him. He told her how to dress, how to act, and what she needed to be in life. He shamed her into sex and refused to be denied. Her family loved him because he was kind and courteous and because Samantha never let on how difficult her life with Tom was. Everyone around her began writing the script for her life, for their life together. At eighteen Tom and Samantha were engaged. It was what everyone expected. It was assumed in the small Oklahoma town they lived in that they would get married, have kids, and settle down as their parents had. It really wasn't up to Samantha at all; the whole town had her entire life planned out for her. And even though she was left crying after her nights with him, he told her he needed her and that was enough to keep her hanging on. When she voiced her doubts about their future, he threatened to kill himself. So she stayed, and her mom planned the wedding while Samantha went along.

Then Samantha left the country for eight weeks of overseas study. Away from Tom for the first time in years and from the suffocating expectations of her small town, Samantha began to think about her life. After the eight weeks were up, she decided to break off the engagement. But it wasn't that easy. Tom was angry, controlling, and manipulative. Her mother and father told her she was throwing her life away. Breaking up with her fiancé involved disappointing her whole family. And they weren't pleased to see her tearing up the script they had carefully prepared for her.

Ten years later Samantha is happily married—to someone she chose, but she still remembers how tough it was to go against the script and break up with Tom. "It was as though I was disappointing my whole family. It was as though I was letting everyone down by not doing what was expected of me. It was the hardest thing I've ever done in my life."

Samantha was fortunate. She realized that others were writing a script for her that featured her in a starring role she never wanted, and she had the strength to back out. Many of us don't. Many of us marry because it is the thing to do, the next thing on the list. You graduate from high school, go to college, meet someone, graduate, get married, have kids, buy a house, and live happily ever after. It is the middle-class thing to do. The pressure these scripts can bring to bear on our lives is enormous. We are forced to live up to society's expectations for us, and woe to the man or woman who fails to live out the script.

Watch any night of television, pick any romance novel, or take home a romantic comedy. In those expressions of popular culture you will find the material with which we create the scripts we then try to live out. We read of men and women being swept off their feet and into whirlwind marriages that last forever (or at least until the last page is turned). We script our life stories the same way, and when reality fails to yield as much drama or as much romance, we alter our views of reality, and we pretend the fairy tale is coming true. We won't even let reality intrude on our precious scripts.

The problem is that one day we wake up and look at the person next to us and realize that the script was woefully inadequate and failed entirely to account for the vagaries of human nature and relationships. Our prince's armor is dulled, the slipper has a crack in it, and we wonder why the script we fashioned so carefully ended before real life even started. Sometimes it is our script, sometimes society's, and sometimes our family's. But the result of marrying because it is the thing to do is the same. We end up disillusioned and disappointed.

We become disillusioned because the reality and the ending that was scripted for us vary so greatly. We've already said that movies and novels end with happily ever after, but real life is only starting at that point. We have envisioned a life of rapture and enchantment, and real life isn't anything like that script we are trying live out. And heaven help the spouse who decides that the role of Prince Charming isn't for him. And not many women can play the ingénue as Cinderella for very long. After a while the kids arrive, and holes in the script appear. When we become disillusioned, we often become angry with our partners, much like Hollywood stars who flub their lines and constantly blame their co-stars for giving them the wrong cues. Since we don't want to fault our script and examine ourselves, we determine that since the fault isn't with the script or us, it must be with our co-star. Because we may doubt that we can ever be happy with him or her, we begin to look for a new leading man or leading lady to play out the drama of the rest of our lives. We are unaware that it isn't the actor's fault and that the fault lies in poor writing—a script that failed to take into account reality.

Judy and I had to deal with the script that others were writing for us, but perhaps the script that was most damaging was the one Judy carried around inside, the one she had been fashioning for years, ever since her father had died.

I was dating the most exciting man in town. People either loved him or hated him. They either felt very safe with him or completely threatened. It was difficult to be neutral about Jerry Schreur. Dating him was good, but I knew I wanted more. In my dream the princess always married Prince Charming. And to me Jerry was Prince Charming. Sure he rode a motorcycle instead of a white horse. Sure his fists were his weapons and he lacked a sword, but he still had the ability to take me away from everything I had known. In my fairy tale Jerry drove up, I jumped behind him on the bike, and we rode off into the sunset. I didn't worry about what happened after that, because in my dream, in my script, happily ever after didn't need any explanation. I would be with him all the time, and he would never let me go.

The holes in my script started to appear when I got pregnant and we weren't married. But I wasn't going to let that deter me. If anything, that helped me in my course of action. Because in 1963 in small-town Michigan you got married when you were pregnant, that was the script the entire town wrote for you. I walked down the aisle three months pregnant, convinced that fairy tales did come true; at least they did for me.

It was only two years later, however, that my script seemed

to have lost its meaning, and I was pretty convinced I had picked the wrong leading man. I had two baby boys and a husband whose mysterious silence that had so entranced me now drove me to distraction because I needed someone to talk to. The same man who stubbornly stood up to the chief of police now stood up to me, and I had never had a man tell me what to do. In my script the last page had me riding off into the sunset. There wasn't anything about overtime at the factory, two crying babies, no money, and a house that was falling apart. Clearly something had gone wrong. I was twenty, disillusioned, and disappointed. And I didn't see any way out.

Often as the script's grip on us erodes, we end up disappointed, wondering why we blithely chose to follow the prepared script, wondering why we were afraid to improvise, and wondering why we never let real life intrude on our fairy tale. Sometimes we end up doubting our ability to make good decisions, while behind the fatalism with which we approach each new day, many of us are intensely weary and want out.

Marjorie's story illustrates another problem with living out the script others have written for us; we become angry with the scriptwriter. "I was dating a guy in college who was really focused on his grades and his future. Compared to the losers I had spent most of my time with, that was a welcome thing. In fact, I let him plan his life and my life. He never even really asked me to marry him; he just assumed I would, and one day we set a date and went shopping for rings. We got married, he went to grad school, and it wasn't until last year, after the last of my kids went to school, that I slowed down enough to pay attention to the emptiness that seemed to be always lurking under the surface. I realize now that I let

David write the script for our lives and for our marriage. He even knew when it was time to have kids; it was written in the script. But now I'm kind of angry, and I don't know where I fit anymore. I just know that I want to live my life, my way. And I'm wondering if he should even be a part of it. Frankly, I find it hard to be in the same room with him. He drove me here. It was his plan, and now I've got nothing of my own."

When the script fails to bring fulfillment, anger at the writer is useful and normal, but it doesn't get to the root issues. We may be angry at our parents, at our church, even at ourselves for writing a script that directed us to this place, seemingly a place without meaning and lacking in romance. In our anger we become irrational. We say and do things that hurt and wound the people who care about us. The simple truth is that lashing out or running away isn't going to help.

A Better Way

We need to create an entirely new kind of script—a script that takes into account real life and real people. We need to work with our spouses to create a script that meets both of our needs and has realistic expectations. We need to understand that disappointment with our mate may just be disappointment with the script we have followed; it isn't anything they are lacking. Nor is it even a lack of love. We are dissatisfied with the script we have been living out. It is time for a change.

What to Do

If you are not married, now is the time to examine the script you are living. Ask honest questions. Why are you in this relationship? Why are you making the plans you are making? Why are you with this person?

If you are married and reading this chapter has struck a chord deep inside, you may be wondering what to do. Maybe you believe your marriage was a mistake because you were just following the script that others had created for you, and now the question is "What do I do? How can I escape?" The answers aren't easy, and there aren't ten steps to total happiness. However, there are some simple things you can do to create a life that brings a measure of fulfillment.

Talk

Rid yourself of the delusions and the illusions that have been twisting your relationship and your hopes and dreams. Instead, talk to your spouse about what you want your marriage to look like. Don't assume that your partner knows what you are thinking. Be honest, be truthful, and be realistic. Create your own script by talking about your expectations. And by the way, the expectation of a totally intimate and romantic relationship isn't realistic. A more realistic expectation might be, "I want to be good friends with my marriage partner." Not enough for you? That is more than many of the people who walk into my office will ever dream of. Since it is a possibility, go for it.

Stay

It is too easy to read a book like this one and find sixty-five reasons to leave your spouse. Maybe you were following the script others wrote for you. Maybe you feel as though you never had a choice and you were just pushed into this marriage. So what! The hard truth is that God expects you and me to make our tough marriages reflections, albeit poor ones, of His love for us. And as much as I have combed the Bible, I have yet to see an easy way out of a marriage commitment.

You followed a script. You married your high-school sweetheart. You put him through college. And now he is not there for you! The kids provide some meaning, but when you head to the movies, you realize that you missed out on the big love, the life-dominating romance. By comparison, your love life, your sex life, your entire family life seems dull and contrived. You realize you've listened to your parents and married the steady guy, the one who puts in a hard day's work but isn't too good with flowers and spontaneity, and now you think the script has led you into a trap and you want out. It is only a trap if you insist on looking at it that way.

Stay and discover the joy of being committed to God's plan. When you stay, you avoid that most seductive of scripts that lays out there. It is a script written by our culture that tells all of us to seek our own fulfillment at any cost and to look to our own needs no matter what wounds we inflict on others in the process. Stay and prove that ordinary love is, in fact, spectacular.

Build

Many people get married for the wrong reasons. Often those marriages become things of beauty. That happens when the men and women in those relationships decide to build on the good stuff and work on what isn't so good. The first and best way to begin that process is to wake up each day committed to catching your spouse doing something right. Look around you at the little things that become big things when taken together. Look at the way she cares for the kids. Look at the funny way he crinkles his nose. Laugh at her inability to tell a good joke. Smile at his inability to stay awake through the entire movie. Recognize what is positive in your relationship and build on that. Make your life together something the two of you can be proud of.

A Last Word on the Subject from Judy

I had a reasons to leave: Jerry was cold sometimes; he didn't tell me enough that he loved me; he could be sarcastic, sometimes even belittling me. I had followed the script, and I had ended up in a tougher place than I had imagined. I had two little boys who needed a home and a husband who didn't seem to need me. I could have left. I thought about it. But I knew what it was like to be abandoned. I remembered the feeling after my dad had died. I didn't ever want to hurt Jerry like that. And what is more I knew that he just didn't know any other way to be married, any other way to be a man. We had some good things going for us. Our sex life was good. (Don't laugh, that mattered a lot to me back then.) He was a hard worker and a good dad. He was getting serious about his faith. He was bright and could fix anything. We had some good stuff to build on. So I stayed, and I committed to finding the best in him every day. Some days I lived that commitment; some days I didn't. But without really knowing it, I had created a new script. Or more accurately, together Jerry and I had written a new script. It was based on honesty and realistic expectations. Thirty-three years later I can tell you: I made the right choice.

Who Writes the Script in Your Life? Checklist

Instructions: Carefully read the following statements. Check (√) the statements that are true of you. Share your responses with your partner. Discuss what implications these responses have on your marriage relationship.

___ I tend to do the socially acceptable thing.

___ It is difficult for me to stand against the crowd.

___ Sometimes I do what others expect, not what I really think is the right thing to do.

___ I have a tendency to please others.

___ I desire the acceptance of others.

___ I try never to displease others.

___ I sometimes find it hard to make decisions myself. I tend to rely on others to make them for me.

___ I am usually submissive to others and to their plans.

___ It's easier for me to follow someone else's script than to write my own.

CHAPTER 6

When His Kiss No Longer Revives You...
Facing the Reality of Boredom and Routine

ow! That first kiss had really been something. Cinderella smiled with the memory. It was like a torrential downpour of passion on her soul. She had literally ached for another kiss when the first one faded. And her Prince had obliged. It had been on her wedding night (this was the Middle Ages, and she was a nice girl, after all), a night that she had dreamed of, a night she had longed for her entire life. A night that had met her expectations! The passion had been so real, an almost palpable presence in their bedroom.

Afterward, they had lain in each other's arms, silently soaking up the presence of the other person. She had been totally content, totally at ease.... Recalling the memory of her wedding night, Cinderella smiled again, this time a little more ruefully. Where had that passion gone? Sure, they still kissed each other, and once in a while they even made love together. But it didn't feel the same. It was as though they were doing what they thought married couples should do, rather than acting out of love, passion, and excitement for the other person.

It wasn't that she didn't love him. It wasn't that she didn't care for him anymore. But the flame was flickering. Actually, she thought, if she was honest, it wasn't even flickering; it had become a dying ember among the ashes. The smile faded, and a sad frown began to spread from her eyes to her mouth as she wondered, not for the first time, what had happened to happily ever after.

Marie's eyes were red with tears. She had worked her way through most of the tissues in my office and still hadn't found a way to staunch the flow of tears. "I miss what we used to have. I miss the laughter and the joy. I miss the passion. I miss the spontaneous things we used to do together. I miss what used to be!"

Marie's tears had come forth in a flood, a surprise to me in a relatively normal "marriage checkup," which is encouraged for all of the members of our church. Something had loosed a torrent of emotion, and from an innocuous conversation, Marie had begun to tell me that her husband and her children weren't enough to keep her in a marriage that seemed to be increasingly loveless. She painted a bleak picture of a family that was just going through the motions. I had asked a few questions, and behind all the tears and fears and dashed dreams there was one thing: Marie was bored with her husband. And she didn't know what to do about it.

A few years ago I stopped off in a little diner in a northern Michigan town for a quick bite to eat. I was on my way to our cottage near there and was anxious to see my wife and grandkids, who were waiting.

I sat down at an empty table, ordered my food, and noticed a man looking my direction. I quickly looked away, hoping I didn't know him and just wanting to eat alone and get out of there. It wasn't to be, however, as the man, a total stranger, asked if he could sit with me while he ate. When he found out I was a family counselor, Don began to share his dilemma. "I don't really know how to say this, but I'm up here by myself, trying to figure out my life." He began slowly, "And what I guess I'm really trying to do is find a reason to stay married. My wife is a great person. She's beautiful, caring, and understanding. But I just don't feel anything for her anymore. She's just not interesting to me anymore."

We talked for a while, and I began to probe a little. It didn't take long before he confessed to an affair with his secretary. "She excites me. She gets my blood pumping in a way my wife doesn't anymore. I don't know why I can't seem to get any feeling for my wife, but I can't. I'm trying to find a reason to stay married, because a divorce will cost me half a million dollars. But I honestly can't find a compelling reason to stay."

"Let me ask you a question," I said. "Didn't you feel the same way about your wife a few years ago that you feel about your secretary now?

"Well, yeah, something like that."

"What makes you think you won't feel the same way about your secretary in five years as you do about your wife now?"

The End of the Affair

The questions Marie and Don raised are vitally important to anyone who wants to stay married and build a lifelong relationship with another

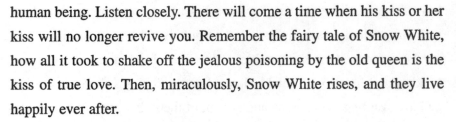

human being. Listen closely. There will come a time when his kiss or her kiss will no longer revive you. Remember the fairy tale of Snow White, how all it took to shake off the jealous poisoning by the old queen is the kiss of true love. Then, miraculously, Snow White rises, and they live happily ever after.

Many of us felt revived by the kisses of our marriage partner. We loved being in love with that person. The sex was intimate and spectacular; the romance made our spines tingle; and each kiss seemed like a new adventure. But it doesn't last forever. By my count I've kissed Judy about twenty thousand times (give or take a few thousand). It isn't the same anymore. Nothing is wrong with Judy, but I honestly know every taste in those lips. I've kissed them when they were barbecue flavored and when they had the remains of spicy Chinese. I've kissed them cold and warm, soft and dry. I've kissed them when she was sad and when we cried for joy. I still like to kiss my wife, but it isn't the same.

One counselor friend puts it this way: "At some point we aren't in the affair anymore. It's just real life, and when it's just real life, it isn't very exciting. When we are dating or newly married, the feelings come in a rush, because we are in a love affair. But those feelings inevitably go away." The question I face in my office every single week, posed by both men and women is this: "What do I do about my changing feelings toward my husband or my wife?"

I think it is instructive to back up a step and ask two other questions: "Why is this happening? Why are our feelings changing?" Answers to these questions aren't always clear to people experiencing (or not experiencing) those feelings. In the last few years I've spent a lot of time dealing with couples in this situation, and there are some common elements to most of their situations.

Newness has worn off

Do you remember that first kiss? What about the first time he or she looked at you and smiled? Do you remember the first night you spent together? All of those moments, so indelibly etched into your memory, are there because they were firsts. It's much harder for me to remember the day after my wedding than it is to remember my wedding. It is much harder to remember my second trip to Hawaii than my first. It's more difficult to recall my third kiss than my first. The very newness of a relationship makes it special. When you share a memorable event with the person you are falling in love with for the first time, it is a remarkably special moment. It is the "first-ness" of it that makes it so very wonderful.

When we meet someone, there are so many things to share with each other. We talk about our life experiences, about our hopes and dreams. We talk about our sorrows and our disappointments, and we listen while they do the same thing. Both of us have an enraptured audience because we are learning about each other. We are discovering things, and that is a remarkable, never-to-be-forgotten time. It does not last forever. Life is not usually a continual succession of firsts. At some point you don't have any new stories to tell. Your partner has heard them all, most of them twice. Your ideas and philosophies no longer sound so smart to him; he's heard them before, and frankly, he's a little bored with them.

Of course, there is always the physical aspect. But even sex, or maybe especially sex, wears thin after a while as well. At first you are exploring your partner sexually. You are learning about him or her, and he or she about you. It is an exciting, fulfilling time. But after a while you've been there, done that. It isn't so new anymore. You know your partner's body, and he or she knows yours. The joy of discovery is gone, and what is left can seem to be a habit.

This desire for newness and for "first-ness" can lead us into big trouble. We'll talk about this in more detail in another chapter, but this desire for these feelings can easily lead us into the arms of another person, because we mistake the thrill of newness for love. This is a key point to remember. When you became attracted and infatuated with the man or woman you chose to marry, part of that infatuation was the newness of the relationship and the joy of the discovery. When that wears off, we wonder where our feelings have gone and why the "mystical spark" is missing. The answer is that it hasn't gone anywhere. The mystical spark never was; it was just the newness and infatuation of the relationship.

Exploration has stopped

Directly related to and a continuation of the first point, we need to understand how the experience of exploring the other person and exploring the world with the other person intensifies our feelings.

I remember rafting down a river a few years ago. It was my first time on the river, and the scenery was beautiful, the weather perfect. Each bend in the river brought magnificent vistas and lush beauty. After the trip was over, I was speaking excitedly with a friend who had accompanied me. The trip thrilled him less than it did me. I said, "Didn't you notice how perfect it was? Didn't you see that eagle in the tree? Weren't you swept along with the beauty of the river?"

"Look, Jerry, I've done this trip many times. All I remember about today were the mosquitoes. I got eaten alive, didn't you?"

Honestly, I can't remember a single mosquito from that trip, but it was my first time. I wasn't looking for the bad things. The things I had never seen before enraptured me. My experienced friend had become jaded, and all he noticed were the bugs.

Our marriages work exactly the same way. In the initial months and even years of exploration the world is new and each bend of the river presents something exciting. But after a while we are traveling roads we have been down many times before. The scenery that once entranced us no longer excites us, and all we notice are the heat and the dust and the bugs.

With couples who are just beginning, it is an exploration of the body, soul, and spirit. It is exciting, fascinating, and revelatory. A new body, with all of its tingling excitement. The soul of a person, the real human being inside the body, is waiting to be discovered and known. And getting to know the spirit of another person, understanding how that person interacts with God, what that person believes, and what that person can teach us are all fascinating to us. Exploration is an exciting and vital part of infatuation. But after a while, you stop exploring, and your partner becomes as familiar as your backyard.

Jerry was a mystery to me. He was tough, yet cried easily at unexpected things. Many people were afraid of him because of his reputation, yet he was gentle with me. Getting to know him after we were married was a great experience. We faced the difficulties of life together, and it seemed as though we could conquer anything. Our lovemaking was special, and I felt very close to him. Our little family grew, and I think I got to a place where I knew Jerry pretty well. I understood his moods without him saying a word, and knew what he needed without being told. I knew how to anger him and how to please him. I learned how to get him to do what I wanted. After a few years we knew each other well. We were done exploring. We had covered everything.

There was nothing new to learn; all the mystery around Jerry had dissipated. Frankly, he was just an ordinary man. I liked the myth I had married a lot better. It was more exciting and romantic.

The chemistry has changed

Judy's story is a good one, because it shows how the mystery can turn into boredom in a hurry, how we marry a myth and then have to live with the real man or woman. One thing Judy alluded to is chemistry. Judy and I always had this chemistry. There was sexual tension when we were in a room together. It scared her mother. It worried my parents. We, of course, loved it. But after a while that chemistry seemed to go away.

Michael Liebowitz, in a pioneering work, *The Chemistry of Love*, explains what really happens, how chemistry, real chemistry, makes it occur. It seems that lovers are quite literally high on drugs. Our bodies are flooded with natural hormones and chemicals that fill us with a sense of expectancy and with a sense of well-being. Harville Hendrix explains the research like this:

> During the attraction phase of a relationship, the brain releases dopamine and norepinephrine, two neurotransmitters. These chemicals help contribute to a rosy outlook on life, a rapid pulse, increased energy, and a sense of heightened perception. During this phase, when lovers want to be together every moment of the day, the brain increases its productions of endorphins and enkephalins, natural narcotics enhancing a person's sense of security and comfort. Dr. Michael Liebowitz takes this one step further and suggests that the mystical experience of oneness lovers undergo may be caused by an increase in the production of

the neurotransmitter serotonin (*Getting the Love You Want*, p. 41).

There really is something chemical that happens when we are attracted to another human being. With continued exposure to the same person, the chemical reaction changes and the relationship literally becomes a duller experience.

What Happens Next?

So you're bored, and his or her kiss no longer revives you. You don't experience that tingle when you catch her eye. His glances of love don't inspire much longing. You make love, but it lacks fire. You hold each other, but it seems to be a function of habit. What happens next?

The answer is up to you. You can, like so many other people, choose to go off in search of the next serotonin high with another person. And you may even find it. But it is inevitable that after the newness wears off and the chemical reaction dulls and the exploring is over that you will then need to leave again and find someone else to stimulate you, to make you "feel" that mystical spark. A friend of mine who chose to come back to his wife and family after a lengthy affair explains his choices rather well: "What was I going to do? Chase after every flutter in my heart. I realized that while I felt good about this person now, that it would take another new person to make me feel the same way. I didn't want to be in a series of relationships, one after another, all of them predicated on my feeling in love. So I went home and asked for forgiveness."

You may, instead, like so many others, choose to try to re-infatuate yourself with your husband or wife. And that may even work for a while. But that will go away as well, and then you are left with the same choice as before, only this time it is more difficult. Because you tried to re-ignite the passion and it failed, you may begin to think just maybe you and your partner weren't meant to be.

I honestly don't think any of us were "meant to be," if by that phrase we mean that there is one person who will fill our days with excitement and love that is never-ending. That fairy tale is responsible for too many divorces. If "meant to be" means a life of exciting, unrelenting intimacy and passion, then Judy and I weren't meant to be.

But if you mean that two people get past the romantic ideal and build a growing and committed love, then I believe in "meant to be." If you mean that a couple, starting with foolishness or dysfunction or escape, can build a strong marriage based on truth and honesty, then I believe in "meant to be." And I really believe this, all of us can be "meant to be."

Cinderella looked at the clock. The prince had promised to be home a half-hour ago. He was often late, always with a good excuse, but inside she was becoming a little suspicious. He seemed to be riding off into the woods often these days, alone. He would leave, and no one would know where he was. She realized their life wasn't exciting, and she had certainly felt stirrings of discontent. She had even felt some illicit pleasure in the barely concealed glances the chief of the guard threw her way. Her heart pounded just to think of him. But she wasn't going to do that to her husband, to her marriage. She wanted to make a different choice; she wanted to choose a grown-up love with her husband. She wanted to talk to him about her boredom and her loneliness, but, well, where was he? The time dragged on...

A Last Word

Don't be the kind of partner who keeps those feelings of boredom and lack of feeling to yourself until one day you leave with just a note on the pillow. If you are bored, if you wonder where the feelings have gone, if you have tried to rekindle the flame and failed, if you have felt the growing attraction to another, do not ignore those feelings and thoughts. Pretending they aren't there will not make them go away. Instead, do at least two things. First, read to the end of this book. Chapters 11–16 will give everyone who wants to build a strong marriage based on truth, not fantasy, some practical help. And second, seek out a trusted, Christian counselor or pastor and begin to ask for help. You aren't going to wake up tomorrow and be "back in love." You need someone you can talk with honestly and truthfully, someone who will encourage you to build a better marriage, a marriage based on something other than changeable, malleable feelings.

Realism and Routine Checklist

<u>Instructions:</u> Check (√) each statement that is true of you. Share with your partner and discuss what the two of you can do to accept the realism and routine in your marriage, while looking for ways to make your marriage more exciting and satisfying.

__ I desire more excitement in our marriage.

__ We regularly explore new areas of life together.

__ We have many activities which we enjoy together.

__ I desire more passion in our marriage.

__ We need to break some of the routines in our marriage.

__ I appreciate the positive routines in our relationship.

__ We are free to take risks together.

__ I could use more discipline in my life.

__ I would like more spontaneity in our relationship.

__ I enjoy our family traditions.

CHAPTER 7

The Empty Castle: Dealing
with the Loss of Intimacy

It was past eleven, and evidently the state dinner still wasn't over. Cinderella liked the wandering magicians who came to the palace, but she resented the time they took away from her family. If it wasn't a state dinner, it was another dragon on the loose or some war to fight. All she had wanted was someone to love her and care for her. Prince Charming was certainly busy, and it turned out that he saved lots of people, and that all took time. They hardly saw each other anymore. What with the kids and the difficulty he was having in running the kingdom, it was a miracle when they had two minutes together uninterrupted. And even then, it wasn't like it used to be.

She had said it to herself and to the royal marriage counselor so many times before: The fire had gone out in their marriage. The passion was gone. She didn't want somebody else, but she did want something different than what she had.

The castle was nice, and servants waiting on her hand and foot was something Cinderella had grown accustomed to rather quickly. But now she thought that she would trade it all for a quiet dinner and some honest intimacy. "Is it wrong to want to be loved? Is it wrong to want to be held?" She thought rather bitterly to herself, "Is it so wrong to want to be remembered once in a while?"

Emptiness = Loss of Intimacy

Perhaps the biggest shock for many of us after we are married is the loneliness that can pervade a house filled with people. We may be prepared for boredom with our spouse; we may successfully fight off the temptation of an affair; but we are surprised by how lonely it can be to be married. Judy discovered this early in our marriage when I was going to school, working full-time, and leading several Bible studies.

I knew he was doing the right thing, and he had certainly turned his life around. Jerry had a dramatic conversion experience, and finding God had changed him profoundly. He was in Bible college now, leading Bible studies on the weekends, and working full-time to pay the bills. I never saw him. We had two boys who missed their daddy, but even more I missed him. I needed him, and he was always gone. I thought that everything he was doing was important, and I didn't dare argue with him about those things. After all, how can you argue with the call of God on someone's life? But I was alone in my home while Jerry was busy, and his busyness was hurting our marriage. Where intimacy had lived, emptiness now reigned. Every good thing was happening, but I was alone.

Judy's feelings are echoed in my office every day. Men and women are in houses filled with people but are living alone. When intimacy dies, we are lonely and afraid. And we'll look anywhere to have that need met.

Intimacy Is?

Intimacy is what most of us lack when we say we don't feel anything for our partners. Intimacy is what many of us crave when we go outside of our marriage to have our needs met. Intimacy is what we desire when we say I do, and the lack of intimacy drives many couples to say I don't anymore. But for all of that, intimacy is not very well understood. Before we go any further, it is probably appropriate to figure out what we mean when we talk about intimacy.

Edward Waring has written some good things on marital intimacy, and his definition of it, while lengthy, is excellent. In his book, *Enhancing Marital Intimacy*, he says that intimacy is a composite of: (1) affection—the degree to which feelings of emotional closeness are expressed by the couple; (2) expressiveness—the degree to which thoughts, beliefs, attitudes, and feelings are communicated within the marriage; (3) compatibility—the degree to which the couple is able to work and play together comfortably; (4) cohesion—a commitment to the marriage; (5) sexuality—the degree to which sexual needs are communicated and fulfilled;

(6) conflict resolution—the ease with which differences of opinion are resolved; (7) autonomy—the couple's degree of positive connectedness to family and friends; and (8) identity—the couple's level of self-confidence and self-esteem (p. 23).

That's a lot to think about, but it helps us understand this thing called intimacy. A different way to talk about intimacy is to say it is the way we are connected to another person, including the meeting of our needs, hopes, and dreams. It doesn't really matter how we define it; the truth is, that without a reasonable level of intimacy, marriages collapse and die. And for want of intimacy people go outside of their marriages for fulfillment and leave their marriages in a search for it. Intimacy is a big deal, and the lack of it even bigger.

Most of us start out our marriages with a reasonable level of intimacy, but somewhere along the way we lose touch, and we drift apart. Not usually in a dramatic fashion, but slowly we begin to go our separate ways until one day we wake up next to a stranger. How that happens can be difficult to say, but researchers have isolated some things that destroy intimacy. Willard Harley calls them love busters. For our purposes these are the things that chip away at intimacy and that erode our attempts at connectedness.

Protection and Withdrawal

Intimacy is killed when, out of a need to protect ourselves, we withdraw from the person we are in relationship with. Instead of being vulnerable and letting our partner look unhindered into our soul, since intimacy really deals with our innermost being, we protect ourselves from pain and withdraw. We literally shut our partners out of our inner lives. We do this for a variety of reasons, but the simple truth is that when we let someone see us for who we really are, we give that person the ability to hurt us deeply. Some of us have been terribly wounded in the past and have been so badly treated that we will never give another person the chance to hurt us that way again. So anytime we feel threatened, we withdraw from the relationship.

Two things grow out of that withdrawal. The first thing that happens is that the other person feels hurt and disconnected. Out of that hurt, that person may lash out at us or in turn shut us out of his or her life. This confirms for us that we have made the right choice in denying that person access into our souls. It is a vicious circle. The second thing that happens is eventually we forget how to open up. We become so practiced, so good at denying anyone entrance that even when we would like to tell the truth about ourselves, even when we choose to let someone in, we can't.

We also withdraw because engagement requires honesty, and we aren't ready for that. In my marriage the hardest thing for me to say is "I'm sorry." I'm embarrassed to tell you how long I was married before Judy heard those words from me. When we would disagree, I would withdraw, because when I withdrew, I didn't have to be honest and admit my failings and my faults. Thirty years down the road I still fight this tendency. My withdrawal has probably caused more struggles in my marriage than anything else. After talking to thousands of men, I am convinced that I am not alone. Many men have the same difficulty. Many of us were raised to withhold emotions. We learned to do that by withdrawing emotionally, which is not a quality that leads to a satisfying marriage.

In his great book, *Inside Out*, Larry Crabb talks about the sin of self-protection. That's right, he goes so far as to say this desire to protect ourselves and insulate ourselves from any pain is a sin. It can certainly become a source of great conflict in your marriage, and the desire to protect yourself and withdraw will destroy intimacy.

Susan was from a large family. She felt left out because she was the only daughter in a family of athletically minded men. It was always difficult for her to connect with her dad; he was from the old school and talked only about the Nebraska Cornhuskers' football team and never about his feelings. Susan learned to hide her emotions and protect herself. She never cried, even when her father died without ever telling her he loved her. After college Susan fell for a man she worked with. They started as friends, grew closer, and began to discuss marriage. When she and I talked, she was just three weeks away from her wedding. But she was afraid. Her fiancé accompanied her, and he was afraid as well. According to them everything was fine until they had a disagreement, and then Susan would clam up and emotionally go away. Her fiancé was from an expressive family where every question was loudly hashed out; it was incredible to him that a person could refuse to argue. It was impossible for him to deal with her when she just, in his words, "went away."

We talked for a long time, and after a couple of weeks Susan began to talk of her past and how she had learned that sharing her feelings was wrong, and how she had lived that way for years. She admitted that she wanted to let her fiancé into her life and usually could. But when they argued, it was as if something snapped in her, and she withdrew from him, like she had withdrawn from her dad for so many years.

Susan and her fiancé were fortunate. They discovered this before they were married and were able to begin to work on it right away. This love buster didn't have a chance to destroy them because they sought help.

Criticism and Contempt

"I didn't really want to leave. But I got so sick of being criticized. I couldn't do anything to please her. There was always something wrong with what I did. I finally stopped trying."

—Leonard

"It got to me after a while. He laughed at me whenever I told him something important to me. He thought I was always being so childish. He made fun of me in front of others. When I told him I was leaving, he was surprised and hurt. He dared to tell me that he loved me and didn't want me to go. I couldn't believe it. After what he had said to me. After the way he had treated me for so many years."

—Amy

"It wasn't so much what he said. It was the way he looked at me. I knew, just knew that I wasn't living up to his expectations. He wanted me to be something I wasn't. I wasn't as cultured as he was. I wasn't even as smart as he was. I mean, he was a doctor, but he let me know in little ways every day that I could never measure up. One day I just quit."

—Marcia

If we wanted to, we could fill the rest of the book with words like those of Leonard, Amy, and Marcia. Men and women kill intimacy in their marriages by their critical words and contemptuous attitudes. These are two major warning signs of a marriage in trouble. In a relationship where criticism and contempt find a home, they quickly chase out any remaining intimacy. Intimacy is fragile and must be nurtured. Criticism and especially contempt will kill it quickly.

When we criticize our spouse, we are spending our time looking for the negative. We are searching for the things that are wrong with our partners or focusing on areas in which we disagree. Then we decide that God has ordained us to let them know what is wrong with them. When we are contemptuous, we do even more damage. Contempt is criticism designed to hurt and belittle the other person. It is often abusive and, without a doubt, in direct contrast to God's imploring us to love our spouse with an unconditional love modeled on His love for us.

Here's a secret that will keep you from destroying intimacy. Your partner already has a fairly good idea what is wrong with him or her. What your spouse lacks is a solid understanding of what is "right" with him or her. In his study on why marriages succeed or fail, John Gottman found that healthy marriages have a ratio of positive interactions to negative interactions between spouses of five to one. In other words, the healthy partners caught their partners doing something right five times more often than they caught them doing something wrong. Do that in your home and experience the positive impact it will make.

It probably isn't news to you that contempt and criticism destroy intimacy. Yet so many of us engage in that kind of behavior. Why is that? There are many reasons, and to pursue that question thoroughly is beyond the scope of this book, but let me say this: If you were raised in a critical environment, then watch and listen to yourself very carefully. Those of us raised in those kinds of families are much more likely to act that way to the people we love and call our partners. Pay attention to your words, for they are extremely powerful. "Death and life are in the power of the tongue" (Prov. 18:21, KJV). Words can build or destroy intimacy.

Insecure people often have a need to tear down their partners, for it is only through the fall of another that they feel built up. If you struggle with insecurity, don't seek the false cure of degrading others. In the long run you will end up alone, and they will end up feeling less human. No one wins. If criticism and contempt characterize your marriage, run, don't walk to a marriage counselor. Get some help, listen to someone who can help you sort through the "whys?" and "why nots?" of your relationship and help you begin to see the positive in your spouse again.

Control and Selfishness

Researcher Karen Kayser found that 53 percent of disaffected spouses, those headed out of the marriage, reported attempts by their partner to control and bully them, which resulted in a turning point in their relationship. The bullied partner decided to move toward divorce.

Recently Judy and I were speaking at a couples' conference in Hawaii. At the end of the first session a man in the audience loudly commented on the worthlessness of the session. "I thought this was going to be a biblical conference where wives would find out their duty is to submit to their husbands." When I asked him what he had expected, he replied, "I wanted you to talk about submission of wives to their husbands, their biblical role." I asked the audience if they wanted to stay to talk about this subject for a few minutes, and they all said yes.

I began by explaining the role of husbands and wives from a biblical perspective. I mentioned rather strongly, but gently, that he should be concerned about his role, and not the role of his wife. I then went on to explain the biblical role of a husband—to love and cherish his wife in a sacrificial way, even as Christ loved the church and gave Himself for it. Of course, he wasn't happy with my answer. So I encouraged him to talk with me privately afterward. He did, for over an hour, still without satisfaction. When I talked to the pastor of the sponsoring church later, I learned that this woman had accommodated her husband in many ways, but he demanded absolute obedience from her and ruled with an iron hand. He literally dominated every aspect of her life. She was getting ready to leave him at that point but was hoping for some answers from the seminar. He too was hoping for some answers, but he mainly wanted support for his iron-handed leadership. To him, marriage was about who was in charge, and he believed that God had told him that he was in charge. Sadly, they never returned to finish the seminar.

I feel bad for this man and even more so for his wife. Research tells us that marriages where power is shared and distributed equally are happier and healthier. When power is shared and nobody seeks to dominate, trust is the result. Trust and a loving intimacy are only possible in that kind of environment. Let me be honest, if partners seek to control their spouses, they are headed for trouble. The only possible outcome to that attempt is anger and frustration. Control results in a loss of intimacy and, too often, the end of the marriage.

A balance of power communicates a sense of equality and respect to each partner in the marriage. Our partners will hesitate to share with us openly if they believe we are trying to control them. It is difficult to be completely intimate with someone who is thinking primarily about himself or herself, and control is at the heart of that person's selfishness. It is a killer of intimacy.

Dishonesty and Mistrust

"I thought we had a good marriage. I know it wasn't without its normal ups and downs, but on the whole it was a good thing. I was devastated when I found out he was having an affair. It wasn't just the thought of him having sex with someone else, although that was hard to take; it was the idea that he had been lying to me. And even when I found out and he supposedly 'came clean,' he still didn't tell me the whole truth. He had been seeing her for over a year. Even after we reconciled the first time, he continued to see her. It wasn't the affair that destroyed our marriage; it was the dishonesty."

Monica's anguish has been repeated in homes around the world. Dishonesty, more than infidelity, anger, or just about anything else, destroys intimacy. Honesty is a basic prerequisite for an intimate relationship. It is the foundational building block. Without it the relationship comes tumbling down. Without honesty, trust is impossible. We will never be intimate with someone we do not trust. How can any of us share our deepest feelings with someone we cannot trust? When we become intimate with someone, we are placing a great deal of trust in that person. When we realize that person is not honest with us, we become afraid of what that person will do with what he or she knows about us. Then trust crumbles, intimacy is gone, and we want out of the marriage.

The Bible tells us to "speak the truth in love," and that we must "put off falsehood and speak truthfully." If you want to create intimacy, you must start with the truth. But that doesn't mean we need to just blurt out unpleasant thoughts or feelings the moment we have them. Michael Morgenstern puts it artfully in his book, *A Return to Romance*:

> "What people have forgotten in the series of 'let it all hang out' explosions we have been through is that honesty doesn't have to mean blurting out the truth in whatever way it comes to you. Honesty involves a choice. You don't choose to express your feelings to a brick wall; you choose to express them to another, living breathing human being, with all of the sensitivity and feeling you have inside yourself. And you can choose, in telling the truth, to be kind (p. 86).

Putting It Together

None of us sets out in our marriages to destroy intimacy. We all want a fulfilling, life-giving relationship that brings joy and satisfaction to both partners. Yet somehow along the way we begin to criticize each other; we stop trusting and start withdrawing. We begin telling little lies, and somewhere along the way we forget that the other person comes first. Instead, our way, our desires, and our selfishness begins to take over. Intimacy dies, we are lonely and wonder what to do. Obviously, the first step is to look hard at the way we interact and to root out, to the greatest extent possible, the intimacy busters present in our relationship. That is a first step.

But often the killer of intimacy is real life. Remember your honeymoon. Remember how close you felt to your partner. How the time you were together seemed to be so perfect. That is because real life didn't intrude. In real life we all work hard. In real life the kids keep us jumping. In real life we get bored and angry and hurt over little things. So the greatest thing you can do to build intimacy into your marriage and to avoid Cinderella's dilemma is to spend time with your partner, learning about each other again, not letting yourselves drift apart. Grow together, learn new skills together, see new movies, eat new foods, and carve out time where for a little while real life doesn't intrude and for just a little while you can pretend the fairy tale is true. Intimacy, while maybe never becoming what you and I wish it would be, can grow. And realize that in the ebb and flow of life it will fade for a while and then come back in a different way. But be patient, wait for it, and be proactive. Don't quit, and don't run away. Stay there.

An Intimacy Exercise for Couples

Instructions: Read the following questions carefully with your partner. Share honestly and positively how you feel about intimacy in your relationship. Complete each question in the order presented. Be creative as you explore new ways (or old ones) of building more intimacy with your partner.

When do you feel the closest to your partner? Where are you, and what are you doing that makes you feel close?

Recall times earlier in your relationship in which you have felt very close to each other. Where were you and what were you doing together?

What was it about those times that made you feel close? Tell each other.

Could you create an environment with some of these same elements today? What would it take? Are you both willing to try? How and when will you begin?

In what areas of life would you like more closeness? Examples: Recreation, Communication, Spiritual, Sexual, Art & Beauty.

Evaluate your closeness to your partner in the areas listed above by writing your initial and the first two letters of each major area listed above on this continuum. Have your partner do the same. Example: If you sense high closeness in the area of art and beauty put your first initial and "AR" on the continuum near the word "High."

|_____|_____|_____|_____|

Low   Moderate   High

Ask your partner what you could do to help him/her feel closer to you in the areas listed above.

What is one action you could take to create more intimacy with your partner?

What is one action you would like your partner to do to create more intimacy?

Defining Intimacy Exercise

Instructions: Carefully read the following definitions of intimacy with your partner. Each choose a definition that you like the best. Tell your partner what you like about this particular definition. Talk together about how you might help each other implement the definitions chosen. If you are into writing, take the best from all of the definitions and with your partner write your personal definition of intimacy.

Definition #1   An intimate relationship is one in which neither party silences, sacrifices, or betrays the self, and each party expresses strength and vulnerability, weakness and competence in a balanced way. (Harriet Goldhor Lerner)

Definition #2   Intimacy is an intensely personal relationship of sustained closeness in which the inner world of each partner is affectionately known and beheld by the other through congruent, empathic understanding, mutual accountability, and negotiability; durable in time yet subject to ecstatic intensification, emotionally warm yet conflict capable, self-disclosing yet distance-respecting. (Thomas Oden)

Definition #3   True intimacy depends on equality. It's a fact that people will hesitate to be completely open with someone whom they perceive as having control over them, or whom they think is in a position to judge them. Nothing is more vital to intimacy than a feeling of equality and acceptance in a relationship. (Joseph Nowinski)

Definition #4   Intimacy in enduring romantic relationships is determined by the level of commitment and positive affective, cognitive, and physical closeness one experiences with a partner in a reciprocal (although not necessarily symmetrical) relationship. (Moss & Schwebel)

Definition #5   Intimacy is a quality of relationship between two people who care deeply about each other, which is characterized by mutual attraction, open and honest communication, commitment to continuation of the partnership, enjoyment of their life together, a sense of purpose for this relationship, and mutual trust which honors and respects each other. (Alberti & Emmons)

Definition #6 Intimacy is an art with as many expressions as there are artists to express it. It is often expressed in the sharing of thoughts and ideas and feelings. It is expressed in shared joys and sorrows, in respect for the deepest needs of the other person, and in the struggle to understand that person. (Source unknown)

Definition #7 Intimacy is the ongoing and painful process of replacing selfishness with love. (*Discipleship Journal*)

Your own definition of intimacy:

CHAPTER 8

The Prince Next Door: Understanding the Lure of Another

$\mathcal{C}$inderella was crying on her royal, four-poster bed. The master bedroom in the castle was larger than the entire house she had lived in prior to the wedding. She had ball gowns and more tiaras than you could imagine. She had servants who dressed her and undressed her. She had people who cut her hair, manicured her nails, and just generally did her bidding. But sobbing into her satin sheets, Cinderella realized that it wasn't enough. She still felt empty. She had been trying to be a good wife. She had really been making an attempt at rebuilding some of the lost intimacy in her marriage. She had even been to the seminar held in the kingdom, "Rekindling Your Dying Flame." It had all been to no avail.

She had stopped seeing the royal marriage counselor. His advice was just too hard to take. But she was lonely, and she missed the romance. In between the sobs Cinderella thought of Prince Eugene. He lived in the castle down the road. Of late they had spent some time riding together. Her own Prince wasn't the slightest bit jealous. He seemed happy just to have her off his hands. Prince Eugene was handsome, although not as handsome as Prince Charming was, but he was a great listener and so thoughtful of her feelings. She had been having some disturbing thoughts about him, and she could hardly even admit it to herself, but she had dreamed about him twice. He was so different from her Prince. Eugene cared about how she was doing, and he didn't spend hours and hours talking about affairs of state. They rode together, and they had so much to talk about. He was a great friend. Maybe even more than a friend.

Cinderella reddened while remembering last night. During their ride, they had stopped to water their horses beside a clear stream. And they had kissed. It had been a good kiss, a surprise kiss, a kiss that reminded her she was a beautiful woman. A secret kiss of passion that she could never share with him again. She was ashamed at the thought of what she had done to Prince Charming, but another part of her felt good. And she cherished the memory even as the shame and guilt tormented her.

It Happens in a Hurry

Cinderella never dreamed that Prince Charming wouldn't be enough for her. On her wedding night she would have dismissed out of hand the idea that anyone else would ever hold any real attraction for her. After all, she was in love, and it was her fairy tale, and they would live happily ever after. But Cinderella discovered what so many of the men and women who have broken down and cried in my office have discovered. When the romantic dream dies, often the lure of another person takes its place.

Shelly was twenty-three when she married Jim. They had a good marriage; Jim was a good guy. He wasn't the most communicative man on the planet, but he loved her in his own way. After a few years Shelly began to want more from Jim. More, in fact, than he could ever give. Shelly wanted him to hold her more, to tell her she was beautiful, and to tell her she mattered to him. But it wasn't his style. At work Shelly had spent a lot of time working with Chad. They were a good team and often found themselves enthused about the same movies and books. One night while working late on a project, they found themselves kissing, and instead of going home they spent the night together in a hotel. Jim believed Shelly when she told him that she had to work so late that it was just easier to grab a room near her office. Now, six months later, Shelly is still involved with Chad. They sleep together infrequently, and by her own admission the sex isn't the main thing. She just feels close to Chad and treasures the intimacy she doesn't feel with Jim. And in my office with tears running down her cheeks, she wonders how this all happened.

Fred isn't a handsome man, but he's funny and warm-hearted. Married for thirteen years with three kids, Fred was a fairly happy family man. His kids brought him joy, but if he was honest, Fred would have to say that he tolerated his wife. She was too serious and way too religious for him. She never smiled anymore and didn't laugh at his jokes the way she used to. She was always trying to drag him to church for yet another special event. It was enough for Fred to go on Sunday mornings.

Three months ago he started a new job. His assistant, Kathy, thought Fred was just about the funniest guy she had ever met, and Fred could feel them growing closer. Kathy was a tall, beautiful blonde—the kind of girl who never went out with him in high school. A month ago she told him that he was attractive and then smiled kind of funny. It made Fred blush thinking about it. He had never considered himself the kind of guy to have an affair. Although he knew it was morally wrong, he found himself hoping that she would come into his office and shut the door. He found himself fantasizing about her. Nevertheless, he made up his mind; he wouldn't have sex with her even if the opportunity presented itself. It would be wrong and unfair to his wife. But last week Kathy did come into his office and shut the door, and they ended up against the wall, kissing and rubbing. In my office Fred is nearly destroyed. He doesn't want to quit his marriage, but Kathy makes him feel things he hasn't felt in a long time. His dilemma is real, should he do what meets his needs or do what he used to believe was the right thing to do?

No One Is Immune

The list of men and women who have sat in my office and told me tales like Fred's and Shelly's is long and filled with people who never intended to have an affair. These people cared about their spouses and their marriages. They never imagined they would find themselves attracted to another person and never imagined they would act on that impulse if it did happen. To them only bad people had affairs, and they knew they weren't bad people. Besides, they were in love, and their marriage would be the one in a million romance that they had hoped for from their teen years.

But something happened, and the romance died, the sex became stale, and anger and conflict and even boredom dominated their lives. Before they knew it, they had created fertile ground for an affair. And then the guilt and shame and impossible choices drove them to despair. The simple truth is that it can happen to any of us.

Learn How It Happens

In twenty-some years of working with couples through literally hundreds of affairs, Judy and I have learned more than a little about the anatomy of an affair. We've learned how they happen and how they can be stopped. It is important to look at some of the reasons good people have extramarital affairs. There are some surface reasons and some deeper, harder-to-get-at root causes. We'll take a few moments to look at both of them, and then help you begin to affair-proof your marriage.

On the Surface

Bill had seen Stephanie three times, and when we met and talked, he was ready to walk away from a four-year marriage to a woman he admitted was "wonderful." Stephanie was beautiful, and Bill was handsome and accustomed to the interest of women, but Stephanie was something special. She looked as though she had stepped out of the pages of the *Sports Illustrated* swimsuit edition. They immediately were attracted to each other, and although he knew almost nothing about her and they hadn't even shared a kiss, he was ready to leave his wife for her.

Attractiveness

The attractiveness of Stephanie was what interested Bill. And although it sounds shallow, that story is repeated too many times. When we feel that chemical rush, reason can be forgotten, and the marriage that may have taken years to build seems suddenly stale and old next to the rush of emotion and desire that we feel whenever we see the person who is inspiring the chemical reaction.

The attractiveness of that person drives us crazy. We compare our spouse to that person, and, of course, our spouse comes up wanting. We think about the person constantly. We fantasize about him or her, our mental imagery taking us where we don't yet dare to go physically.

The funny thing is that we know that physical attractiveness is a shallow thing, and we realize on one level how foolish we are being, but on another level we don't care. I've seen men walk away from their families and their careers because of the beauty of another woman. And women aren't immune. When I talked to a forty-ish woman not long ago about her recently ended affair, she was still gushing inappropriately about the body of her former lover.

Attention

It isn't just physical appearance that causes us to leave our families. Affairs often start as the result of the attention we receive from another person. The typical story is very similar to Cinderella's at the beginning of this chapter. If your marriage is dying and your home is a lonely place, you are susceptible to the attention of another person. It wasn't long ago when I talked to a friend whose marriage had barely survived his affair. "Jerry, I hate to admit it, but I just wanted a woman to pay some attention to me. Janine [his wife] was always so busy with the kids and with her own job. Well, it seemed like I always came last. But with Brenda I was first. She listened to me, she helped me, and she cared about my career and my problems. I loved the attention—that was the trap for me."

The attention we get from another person is all the more alluring when it is someone we spend a lot of time with. A coworker who seems to appreciate us more than our spouse. A friend from church with whom we work closely. A person who values our opinions. Or a neighbor who is available when our spouse isn't, just to talk and to listen and to care.

Alternative

When our marriage is a difficult and dark place, when our future with our spouse seems bleak, any alternative to the present looks good. Nothing can be as bad as the relationship we are currently trapped in. Nothing could hurt more than our current circumstances. The alternative, even if it doesn't seem like a good one at first glance, looks mighty promising.

Rene's story is instructive for us in this regard. "Things got really bad with Michael. He was often angry with me for no apparent reason. And when he wasn't angry, he ignored me. I was lost and lonely. Greg wasn't particularly attractive, and I never felt any grand passion for him, but when we were together, it was an escape from Michael. Even if it wasn't real, it was a pretty good alternative. Or at least it seemed like that at the time."

Admiration

"I admired Frank. It wasn't hero worship or anything, but I saw how he helped others. I listened to him preach every Sunday. He seemed to really understand what God was saying in the Bible. He told great stories and seemed to have it all together. I genuinely admired him. I started hanging around the church, helping out a lot. I just wanted to be with him, to kind of let him mentor me. I never intended to fall in love with him, much less have a long-term affair. But that's what happened."

Jillanne's story is familiar. A person we admire and look up to seems like a welcome change from the all-too-human person we married. Admiration is one of the major reasons we have affairs with our pastors, our bosses, entertainers, and educators. We look up to them, we admire them, and we are flattered and thrilled by the attention they pay us. It is all too easy to become infatuated with this ideal, thoughtful person, who so easily outshines our marriage partner.

A Deeper Level

Those are surface issues that draw us to another person. But underlying those surface issues and often the real impetus behind the transfer of affection are deeper, more profound issues.

Vulnerability

Experts use this word to describe the things that make us fertile ground for an affair. Many things cause this vulnerability, but in our experience we have noticed some recurring themes.

Emotional distancing. Either on your part or on your partner's part, emotional distancing can be a sign of vulnerability. And it doesn't have to be intentional. Sometimes the demands of work and family leave little time for a married couple to build their friendship. One or both partners may feel that they are drifting apart. Often afraid or insecure, they begin to distance themselves emotionally from their partners. It is common. It happens all the time in every kind of relationship. And it leaves us vulnerable to an affair.

When our marriage feels lifeless and the fairy tale is over and the romance is gone, the distance we feel from our partner can seem like an unbridgeable gulf. It is all too easy to find comfort and emotional intimacy in another person.

Invalidation. We feel invalidated when our hopes, dreams, thoughts, and fears aren't listened to, or are ridiculed or belittled. When our partners reduce the meaning of what we care about and our interests have no value for them, then we feel invalidated. We are vulnerable to someone who values what we value and tells us. We then begin to share interests and to share intimately with the other person. It isn't a big step when we wake up one day in the middle of an affair. It is a series of small steps, building intimacy with someone who values our thoughts and who holds our dreams and our hopes as dear as his or her own. We find value and worth with that person, and we are vulnerable.

Continual conflict. When our marriages are not safe places of refuge from a difficult world, and when instead they are places where we always have to be on our guard and fearful that what we say or do may start a fight, we are vulnerable. Continuous conflict wears us out, even if we are the primary instigators. It is no fun and really quite debilitating to live in a constant state of warfare and tension with our partner. An affair becomes a place of rest and escape. It is a place where we can pretend for a little while and get away from the raised voices and the icy glances and stares. We are vulnerable because we aren't prepared to spend all of our days in constant battle with our partner. A person who will hold us and whisper to us that everything is OK becomes a refuge from the turmoil. It is too easy to fall for the prince next door when the one you live with is the enemy.

Unmet needs. "I didn't ever think I would be the kind of guy who had an affair. I mean, I loved my wife, although our marriage had certainly become less exciting over the years, and I'm the kind of person who needs a lot of affirmation. It isn't easy to admit it, but I need a lot of support. My job is pretty demanding with high pressure, and I face a great deal of rejection. It seemed as though my wife had time and attention for everyone but me. When I started working with Susan on a project at church, she seemed to admire me and look up to me. She told me often that I was smart and talented, and I knew she meant it. It seemed natural to call her when I felt down, and natural for her to give me a quick hug goodnight. We were good friends. But one night I hugged her and didn't let go."

Roger's story is a story of unmet needs that left him vulnerable to an affair. His wife, concerned with the very real difficulties of her own job and being a mom, didn't have time to stroke Roger's fragile psyche. When he found someone who had the time and the inclination to do that, it was easy to have an affair, and then it was easy to walk away from twelve years of marriage. In his words, "My wife could never give me what I needed. I wanted and really needed a lot more than she was capable of giving me. I know it sounds callous, but I had to think of me and my own needs for once."

To deny that all of us have needs that we look to have met in our marriages is to ignore the basic facts of why we got married in the first place. What we call love is often just that we have found someone who pushes all the right buttons. We found someone who meets the needs we feel most deeply. That works for a while, but our needs evolve, and when our marriages don't keep pace with that evolution, we are vulnerable to an affair.

Lack of self-esteem. We are also vulnerable when we lack the stability and judgment that come with a healthy sense of who we are. When we feel inadequate, we are vulnerable to an affair because the fact that someone wants to be with us, even if it is only sexually, makes us feel valuable. This lack of self-esteem is rarely the only factor that leads us into an affair, but when you couple it with invalidation or an emotionally distant marriage, then you have a person who is ready and maybe even looking for the prince next door. Developing a healthy, adult identity is one of the

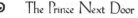

best preventive measures we can have in our marriages. Quite simply, we are less vulnerable when we are confidently aware of the special person that God has made each of us.

Mutual sharing

We fall for the prince next door when our marriages are merely flickering flames, and we find that the prince next door cares about the same things we care about. When we share our lives together and find things in common, that is an exciting time in the development of a friendship. And when the friendship involves a male and female, it is a time when romantic and hormonal feelings begin to invade the friendship.

Let me be clear here: Healthy male-female friendships are valuable. But extreme care must be taken, and the boundaries must be clearly defined. A good friend of mine has a married female as one of his best friends. But early in the relationship they defined what was acceptable and not acceptable. They did this before there was any hint of their friendship getting out of control. And then this friend did a wise thing; he worked hard to build an equally strong friendship with her husband. Boundaries are vital, and if we don't erect them carefully, the mutual sharing could lead to big trouble with the prince next door.

The arc of an affair is easy to predict, and after twenty-five years of counseling hundreds of men and women who are involved with someone they aren't married to, the story is all too familiar. It begins innocently, with a mutual interest or work. Then the emotions are shared, and we begin to think, "Wow! This person really understands me. And they care about me." We begin to compare the emotional sharing to that in our marriage, and our marriage is the poorer in comparison. The newness of the emotional sharing excites us, and we find ourselves drawing closer to that person. We begin to share intellectual pursuits, reading the same books and discussing deep thoughts and ideas. Often we find someone who shares our ideas of art and beauty. We like the same music, and we may have found the only other person in the world as crazy about Jackson Pollock's later paintings as we are. We do things with that person, sharing workouts and recreation like golf or tennis. All the while the mutual sharing is deepening the relationship and drawing us closer together. At some point we realize that we are closer to this friend than we are to our spouse, but instead of alarming us that thought is almost comfortable. It is a secret pleasure, our ace in the hole if our marriage were to continue down the path toward emptiness.

The problem is that while we are putting all our time and energy into this friendship, we aren't putting time and energy and honesty and sharing into our marriage. It is inevitable that the new relationship will feel more exciting and more interesting. It is inevitable that our marriage will suffer in comparison. It is almost inevitable that without firm boundaries and careful accountability, that friendship will bloom into an affair.

If you learn one thing from this chapter, learn this: Affairs are not about sex. They are about inappropriate intimacy with another person. The sexual expression of the intimacy is just a by-product. The real culprit behind the affair isn't the physical expression, although that is often how we characterize an affair. The real culprit is the intimacy that robs our partner of what is rightfully theirs.

Emotional immaturity

When Margo married John, she was twenty-one and he was twenty-five. They had met through a mutual friend, and Margo marveled at John's worldly wise ways. He knew fine wines; he watched foreign movies; he had a real career; he was, in fact, so very different from the fraternity boys she had been dating. When she married him, she felt as though she had really grown up and arrived. Now, six years later, Margo misses her carefree days. She misses the parties and just hanging out with her friends. She misses being a little crazy and just letting loose. Leaving John seemed like a good way to go back to the good old days of adolescence. So she did.

The third thing that leads us into the arms of the prince next door is emotional immaturity. Some people seem to move from childhood to adulthood and skip right over adolescence. Sometimes they are forced to take care of others and become almost a parent in the home; sometimes they latch onto an older man or woman and become instant grown-ups by association. Whatever the reason, the time comes when they resent their partner for making them grow up too fast and they miss the carefree joy of their youth. When the prince next door comes knocking with the promise of a good time and no responsibility, they are only too eager to head out the door. Since their rather staid and dull suburban existence looks pretty boring by contrast with a college frat party, they head out the door.

What Not to Do

You may have read the past few pages with a growing realization that you are vulnerable to an affair. You may have read the last few pages and realized you have a friendship that is becoming inappropriate. You may have read the last few pages in disbelief, thinking that these things could never happen to you. Whatever you think of this chapter, realize this: Never underestimate the need for intimacy. We crave relationships with other people, and we will go to extraordinary lengths to have our needs met. Look carefully at your life, and assess your vulnerabilities and the weak spots in your defenses. If I have learned anything in my years of working with couples, it is that no one, not you, not me, not our partner is immune to the lure of another.

You've seen a litany of what not to do in this chapter. Through the stories of real people with all too real choices you have caught a glimpse of your own choices and perhaps their consequences. If you are in an affair, get help now. Find a Christian counselor and come clean. Tell the truth, the whole truth to him or her. End the affair, and do it with your counselor or a trusted friend in attendance for acceptability. If you find yourself thinking a lot about the prince next door because your prince or your princess isn't meeting your needs and the fairy tale has ended in your castle, work for a different kind of marriage. Work for the kind of marriage we are going to advocate and help you build in the next few chapters. The prince next door is never the answer to your dreams.

Vulnerability Checklist

<u>Introductions</u>: Respond to the following statements thoughtfully and honestly. It is not necessary to share your answers with your partner at this time. If your answers bother you, you might share that concern with your partner. Example: "Some of my answers to this exercise trouble me. I may be more vulnerable than I thought. I'm concerned about protecting and building our relationship. Could we talk about this together? Or, could we talk with our pastor or a counselor?"

Use this scale to answer the following questions:

0 = Not true of me   1 = Slightly true of me   2 = Very true of me

Note: "Another person" is assumed to be a person of the opposite sex.

___ I am strongly attracted to another person.

___ I am giving a lot of attention to another person lately.

___ I really admire a particular person.

___ Another person is expressing strong admiration for me lately, and I find myself liking it and responding to it.

___ I sometimes think of another person as an alternative to my marriage partner.

___ I often feel emotionally distant from my partner.

___ My partner often says things or does things after which I feel less valuable.

___ My partner and I seem to be in continual conflict.

___ My partner seems uninterested in attempting to meet my needs.

__ My self-esteem hovers between low and very low much
   of the time.

__ I never had a chance to really live out my adolescent years.

__ I am spending a lot of time with another person lately.

__ Lately I am very critical of my marriage partner.

__ I often complain about my partner to another person.

__ More and more I find myself sharing openly with
   another person, and they with me.

Scoring: Total your score. A score of 0–10 indicates a normal level of vulnerability, 11–20, a moderate level, and 21–30, a high level of vulnerability. Remember, everyone is somewhat vulnerable to the Prince/Princess next door. If your total score was less than 10, take a look at your responses, especially the "very true" responses. Do some of them cause you or your marriage partner concern? Should you exercise more caution in your relationships outside of your marriage? If your total score is between 11 & 20, you are very vulnerable to the Prince/Princess next door. Take steps immediately to change or stop the relationship. If this is difficult for you to do, or you find yourself getting defensive about the relationship, it probably means there is a strong emotional bonding between the two of you, which indicates high vulnerability. If your total score is above 20, talk to a counselor ASAP to express your concern and get the help needed to break off the relationship and strengthen your marriage.

CHAPTER 9

Cinderella's Discovery:
When He Wasn't What
You Thought He Would Be

he list was getting longer, and Cinderella had no idea what to do about it. The fact was, she was getting royally sick of her Prince. He really wasn't at all what she had expected. Of course, she thought to herself, what had she really expected? It wasn't as if she had given the whole matter a lot of thought, particularly with that whole scene with the glass slipper, running away as the clock struck twelve, and her carriage turning back into a pumpkin. And then all she had left was the memory of the dances they had shared and the thought that she would never see him again. Until the next day, when after an entire night of scouring the kingdom, he had found her. They lit-

erally rode off into the sunset. Who gives a lot of thought to the kind of person they are marrying when it all seems like such a dream? Of course, he would be the perfect prince, and she would be the perfect match for him. Thinking back made Cinderella wince in shame. How could she have been so naive?

The truth was that the Prince wasn't really what she thought he would be. Her annoyance started with his habits. He never polished his armor. He would return from a battle with a dragon and with the green blood of the dragon smeared all over his breastplate. Prince Charming would just drop it on the floor and run to her, expecting a kiss. It was disgusting, and it was rude. It took a lot of hard scrubbing to get that nasty dragon blood out of the carpet.

And then there was his need for physical contact. He was always touching her. After a boar hunt, sweaty and grimy from the ride, he would rush into their room and kiss her without asking, holding her tightly against him. What she wanted was for him to let go and take a bath. But what really bothered her was the obsessive attention he paid to his sword. He polished it until he could see his face in it. Then he would polish it some more. He carefully wiped down the scabbard every night, even taking a cotton swab to the jewel-encrusted case to get every speck of dirt out. If the Prince paid half as much attention to Cinderella as he paid to his weapon, their marriage would be a much happier place.

But his habits weren't the most surprising thing about him. What surprised Cinderella the most was how moody her Prince had turned out to be. The reason he was always riding into the woods was because he was so restless and always in search of someone else to rescue. He could be totally uncommunicative when he focused on something or when one of his black moods struck him. It was as though he didn't know her, and she didn't have any idea how to reach him.

The frustrating part about it was that her uncertainty about his moods and where he was all the time made her distrust him, and she could feel what that lack of trust was doing to their intimacy. Sex wasn't the same, *and his kisses no longer had the same effect on her. She wondered again whether her fairy tale was over, and why she couldn't ever recall what happened after happily ever after.*

What You Don't Know Can Hurt You

Cinderella was coming to grips with one of the most talked about and least understood difficulties of marriage. Most of the time following the moments when we pledge our faith and say I do, we really have a very skewed understanding of our marriage partner. We have an image of them that is made up of how we see them, who they actually are, how they want us to see them, and who we hope they are. Often the result is that we get someone who is very different from that which we had planned and envisioned. It isn't usually a matter of deceit or an intention to pretend to be what we are not. It is just that during the attraction and infatuation stages of our courtship we are careful not to show our negative characteristics. We carefully and often subconsciously try to be the kind of man or woman we think the other person wants us to be.

Personality traits that surprise us

When Debbie met Hans, she thought she had found the man of her dreams. A native of Austria, Hans was charming, gentlemanly, and seemed not to lack money. He bought Debbie expensive gifts and treated her as if she were a princess. They dated for over a year before deciding on marriage. She really loved him, and he loved her. What could go wrong? Just about everything. The one thing they had neglected to talk about, the one thing they had forgotten to find out, was each other's expectations for marriage.

Hans expected Debbie to stay home and make babies; he would do the providing for the family. The trouble with that was that Debbie loved her job and found great value in her work. Debbie's words to me were, "I had no idea he was so old-fashioned, and so controlling. It's like a flash-back from the fifties. He literally wants me barefoot and pregnant. What am I going to do?"

When we are dating and infatuation and attraction are working their way with us, we don't really want to know the entire truth. We want to believe this other person is what we believe him or her to be. We don't want to have to live with the knowledge that there might be something more, something we have missed. And when we find out there is some-thing more, we are often bitterly disappointed, both in our partner and in ourselves for not being wiser and asking for more honesty up front.

It is very difficult to be objective about someone who thrills you with his kisses or inspires you with her looks of love. But when the attraction becomes commonplace and the infatuation fades, then the objectivity comes in, and we end up looking with open eyes at someone we knew but never really saw before.

In short, we date a persona, but we are married to a person. The dif-ference is profound and must be understood. It isn't that our partners have deliberately tried to hide their real selves from us. They have done exact-ly what we all do. They have projected the best for public view, and it was the best of them that we fell in love with. That part doesn't usually go away. What usually happens is that we discover that the part that we love so dearly is merely part of a much larger whole. We discover the person underlying the persona. And sometimes that discovery is a bit of a shock.

Values that aren't what we had hoped for

It isn't just personality traits that surprise us. I am always struck by how many men and women come into my office and talk about how surprised they are by the values of their spouse. It is possible to marry someone without really knowing his or her values. It is possible to marry someone and yet not really understand what motivates them, what moves them, what makes life interesting and meaningful for them. Our values aren't just our religious beliefs or even our morality. They are all-encompassing including things like security, freedom, pleasure, recognition, art, and beauty.

Bill and Sandy are an example of what can happen to a couple who never understood that they held different values. Sandy was taken by Bill's intelligence, and he loved teaching her about the things that mattered to him. It was fun to talk with her about books he was reading and how he loved the architecture of Philip Johnson and Frank Lloyd Wright. She listened, learned, and found this aspect of Bill's personality engaging.

Nevertheless, after they were married, his almost total absorption in art and literature surprised her. He would tune her out for what seemed like days on end while reading a novel of great power and beauty. He would sit and look at a painting without saying a word, transfixed for forty minutes. She was bored with the whole scene, and he became resentful of her. She didn't care about what he cared about. When he spoke about seeking beauty and finding truth, she didn't have any idea what he was talking about and thought he was pretentious. When she shut him down in his search for beauty, he thought that she lacked the appropriate sensibilities and that she was shallow. Art and beauty were things he valued and was moved by. Sandy could appreciate a good painting, but it never moved her. Their values were different, and the depth of that difference surprised and saddened both of them.

Family dynamics

"If I had known how messed up Jennifer's family was, I never would have married her." Jonathan's words were almost spit out in anger. It seemed that the mistakes that had haunted her parents were being repeated in his own marriage. In fact, his wife, insecure and needing love, yet withdrawn and afraid after an abusive relationship with her father, had just left Jonathan. She had married him hoping for something he couldn't provide—the end to her insatiable need for male approval.

Jonathan had fallen in love with a beautiful, funny, and caring woman. Her family lived miles away, and sure, they were a little strange, but they didn't see them much, except when he began to see them every time Jennifer and he disagreed about something. She would move from abusive anger to complete withdrawal in minutes, emulating her own mother's survival mechanism in a dysfunctional family.

Jonathan was serious. When the extent of the dysfunction in her family began to haunt his own, he wondered why he hadn't explored her past more thoroughly, hadn't looked more closely at her mom and dad, and hadn't noticed that every one of her brothers and sisters were either divorced or headed in that direction.

We come into our marriages carrying an enormous amount of baggage from our families of origin. And it isn't just about dysfunction. We carry the family traditions and expectations. We carry the ethnic heritage and the generational struggles. We carry the past experiences, good and bad, that shaped our family; and although we don't say it, we all believe our family was normal. And that is because it is all we knew. So we assume that while other families may do things differently, they can't be all that different, and that our family did things the right way. Of course, after a few months of marriage we find out that all of those little illusions aren't true.

Mike met Ronda in Europe. They spent almost six months in Paris together, and they fell in love. Ronda came home from France engaged, and although Mike noticed that her family wasn't exactly fond of him, he didn't take it too much to heart. Moreover, although he noticed that sometimes Ronda would withdraw from him briefly, disconnecting for a time and seemingly depressed, he figured it would be OK. After three years of marriage he realized something—Ronda's family had hurt her deeply, and she was still wounded by her experiences. The happy, carefree girl he had met and loved in Paris was a moody, depressed, and sometimes angry person. While determined not to give up on her, he wondered where it all came from. They went to counseling together, determined to try to work out their problems. Only in therapy did Mike realize how deeply scarred Ronda was by her family and how much those wounds affected his own marriage.

What you don't know about your partner can and maybe will hurt you. What you don't know about your partner's personality traits may surprise you and confuse you, leaving you to wonder if you have been deceived. What you find out about his or her values may mystify you, because you are moved and touched by very different things. And what you don't know about your partner's family background may haunt you. It isn't a platitude; it is truth when the Bible tells us that the sins of the fathers are carried to the third or fourth generations. What we have seen and what we have experienced in our families cannot be adequately told or explained to our partners. Often we are ashamed of it and don't want to talk about it, but it does affect us, and it can hurt our marriage, all because it turned out that our prince isn't what we had hoped he would be.

What You Do Know Can Irritate You

"I really loved Eric's generosity. He never passed a homeless man without buying him some food. He never failed to help someone in need. He gave of his time and his money so generously. It was one of the things I found so endearing and attractive when we were dating. He's still generous, but it really bugs me now. Our money is tight, with the kids needing new clothes, and Eric doesn't make a lot of money in his job as a youth pastor. Things are tough but he still gives to anyone who asks him. If all the kids who owed him money from his youth group paid him back, I probably wouldn't have to worry about paying the rent this month. And yesterday he came home and told me that he had given a family in our church our extra car. It was a junker and barely ran, but it was my only transportation when Eric is gone. And he just gave it away. 'Why do we need two of something that another family doesn't even have one of?' he said to me. I was so angry I spent the night with friends. I don't know how we are going to make it."

Too much of a good thing

We marry our partner because we see some things in our partner we like and admire. They have characteristics we wish we had or that we find attractive. But after a few months or years of marriage, those characteristics seem to be flaws. In fact, they are too much of a good thing. What we used to see as generous now seems irresponsible; what we used to see as reflection now seems merely moody.

Before we were married, we only had to deal with these dominant characteristics in small doses. Then we admired that assertiveness and leadership. But when we became a partner with them in marriage, the dosage is radically increased, and what used to be attractive and positive becomes a source of irritation.

Habits we used to tolerate

"His smoking wasn't a big deal, until he upped it to two packs a day. Every time I looked at him, he had a cigarette in his mouth. It got so that I wouldn't even kiss him. It was repulsive."

I remember one Christmas, maybe six years into my marriage, I had picked out the perfect gift for Judy. I love my wife, but sometimes her organizational skills are not up to my standards. So I carefully shopped and found just the right thing for my lovely bride. I purchased turntables that would fit inside the cupboards and organize them nicely for her. She seemed a bit taken aback when she opened the gift, but nothing prepared me for the tears that followed later that night. She said, "You just don't care about me at all. You want to turn me into something I'm not, and you don't love me anymore. How could anyone buy their wife Rubbermaid turntables for Christmas?" I had honestly thought I had done pretty well. I was just trying to help.

By then I had just about had it up to here with Jerry's need for organization. I mean whatever happened to just living a little bit. The last straw was those stupid turntables. I was ready to have him wear them. In the end I got my revenge. I loaded them up with so many things they wouldn't turn, at all. Jerry just shook his head in dismay.

My habit of organization, formerly tolerated, became a serious problem in our marriage, contributing to a lack of intimacy and togetherness.

Behavior you assumed would change

Many of us marry our partners knowing there are things we don't especially appreciate about them. They are obsessed with cars, with clothes, or with their looks. But we feel that we are strong, that we can change them, and that, in fact, we can make them more like us. And sometimes that does happen. But just as often, they become more ingrained in their annoying habits.

The football-loving husband watches both college and the pros and then heads out to a friend's house every week for the Monday night game. The wife who loves to party with her friends ends up leaving her husband home alone four or five nights a week because he prefers to read and relax. He resents any time away and was convinced he could show her how enjoyable it was to just sit. But she tried that, and it bored her. So she is gone more than ever.

We tolerate certain behaviors from our partners because we think that after marriage they will change or we will be able to change our partner. Now you realize you will never change the other person and this irritates, frustrates, and angers you. They disappoint you because they don't change; you can't change them, your goals are blocked, and you are angry. Plan A doesn't work; Plan B doesn't work; now you are on Plan H, but nothing works to change your partner. You get more and more frustrated—you probably should have known that a person can change only himself or herself, not others.

I was so sure I would be able to change Jerry after we were married. I just knew I would be able to convince him to comb his hair after riding in a convertible. But to this day Jerry combs his hair only in the morning, even if we go to church with the top down. Then he proceeds to spend the rest of the day without a comb. Mirrors didn't help; strategically placed combs didn't help; and nagging got nowhere. This was and is a major issue for me, a person whose hair doesn't just blow but lifts in sections because of the hair spray.

And then there is the issue of table manners. I grew up in an environment where table manners were important, but in Jerry's large family it was first come first serve. I often made and still do make positive suggestions on proper etiquette. Did I succeed? Come for dinner some evening, and you will be able to witness firsthand my acute failure.

When we fail in our attempts to change our partner, we become frustrated, and the things that bother us that we cannot change seem to grow in importance, until the negative qualities far outweigh whatever good we used to see in our partner. When couples like that come into my office, their refrain is nearly identical: He's just not what I hoped he would be.

What You Become Can Disconnect You

Perhaps the most difficult thing to deal with in marriage is the inevitable changes that occur in each of us over a lifetime. Marriage is supposed to last forever, but the person we married is usually a very different person in just three or four years. And, of course, we aren't immune to change ourselves, becoming and growing as well. The end result is that we can become disconnected because we are not what we used to be.

Many couples use this reasoning as an escape hatch. One woman said to me, "I'm not the girl he married. He isn't what I need anymore, and I'm not what he wants anymore. The best thing I can do is leave." While I disagree with this woman's conclusion, I think she has hit on some key issues.

Our needs change

We get married because our partner meets some deeply felt needs. And in having some mutual needs met, we begin to fall in love. All of that is well and good, except what happens when our needs change? What happens when you no longer need to be nurtured back to emotional health, but instead you need freedom to fly on your own? What happens when you need more intimacy and less space, but your partner has no idea or even the inclination to try to do that? What happens when you married someone because you were lost and looking for direction, but now you want to make your own choices and rise and fall on your own merits? What happens when you married someone who was committed to making money and rising in the work world, just as you were, but you want out of the fast lane, and he or she show no signs of tiring?

Our needs change as we grow and change. All of our experiences and our education, both formal and informal, contribute to making us very different people from who we were when we first met. And in that difference conflict arises and we desire to escape, to get out to start anew, because our spouse isn't what we hoped he or she would be.

Our values change

Values, although often discussed as if they were written in stone, do grow and change, and sometimes that puts us in a very different place from the person we committed to in marriage. One couple I know is experiencing severe difficulty because she just converted to Catholicism and he doesn't believe. Their values are on a collision course, and they are wondering how they can reconnect. Values are what make us who we are; they are what drive our ambitions, our hopes, and our dreams. When we disconnect around values, we are going to suffer some difficulties. Values matter. They are about who we are at a basic level and who we want to become.

Brian told his wife, Jill, something interesting during one of their increasingly common fights: "I will never give up on our marriage, but I will never give up on who I am either. I just can't become what you want me to be, because that wouldn't really be me. It would just be me pretending for your sake. I can't do that. And you'll have to accept me for what I am, right now, and then do that all over again in five years when I'm someone different."

Our family dynamics change

Nothing brings more radical change to a marriage relationship than children. When you invite children into your life, you have just completely and forever altered the dynamic between the two of you. Because it isn't about the two of you anymore; it is now about the three or the four or even the seven of you. And in that one change, adding a child, an entirely new set of value propositions must be dealt with, and with that new set of value propositions comes an enormous number of opportunities for conflict.

The Inevitability of It All

Change isn't something you can prevent or ignore. All of us will become different people as the years go by. And that is a good thing. Remaining stagnant and refusing to grow isn't healthy or attractive. But growing always entails the risk of growing apart and becoming people

who no longer like each other. Every marriage reaches a point where both partners have to be willing to make some very difficult choices if they are going to stay connected in the midst of this great change in each other. Every marriage demands a level of commitment in spite of this change that doesn't come easily.

He Can't Be What You Thought He Would Be

Our husbands and our wives will surprise us with things we wish we didn't know. They will grow and become people we like less. They will do things that drive us crazy, and even the things we find endearing may begin to wear on us. Underneath it all is the complaint, heard around the world, my partner isn't the person I thought he or she was. Or, my partner has become someone I no longer like and or wish to be with.

In the last six chapters of this book, we are going to talk deeply and meaningfully about the choices you have when you get to this point. So for now let us say one thing: Count on some other things you read about in this chapter happening, because they will. Don't be surprised to wake up next to a stranger who you have lived with for years. But don't quit at the point. Stay, learn, grow, adapt, and become. We think you can do it.

Expectations, Irritations, and Disconnections Checklist

Instructions: Read the following statements carefully. Check only the statements that are true of you. Discuss your responses with your partner. How do some of these items affect your relationship? Are there some changes you should make to adapt to the disappointments and things which may have cause you to disconnect with your partner? What can you personally do to make the adjustments needed?

__ Some of my partner's personality traits have surprised me.

__ Some of my partner's values are quite different from mine.

__ Our family dynamics from our families of origin sometimes trouble me.

__ Some of the things I used to admire in my partner now seem like too much of a good thing.

__ Some of my partner's habits which I used to tolerate now irritate me.

__ I thought my partner would change his or her behavior after marriage, but that hasn't happened yet.

__ My needs have changed a lot since we were married.

__ Some things which were once important to me are no longer important. It seems that other things have taken their place in order of importance.

_ Our family dynamics have changed a lot since we got

married.

We hope awareness of differences will lead to acceptance of those differences, adaptation to those differences, and appreciation of those differences. Differences can complement a relationship and make it stronger. At some point you might move beyond appreciation to admiration of your partner as you see his or her uniqueness and begin to sense something of the wonder of God's special creation (Ps. 139:13-16) as you see your partner from another perspective.

CHAPTER 10

Cinderella's Longings:
When He Doesn't Fill the
Hole in Your Soul

━━━◅▻━━━

I t wasn't that the Prince was a bad guy. He had turned out to be
something a little more austere and formal than she had antic-
ipated, that was true. But he was a good man. It was just that
even in her marriage, Cinderella lacked a feeling of complete-
ness. It was as if there were still a big part of her life missing.
The royal marriage therapists insisted on calling this yawning emptiness, "the hole in your soul." And Cinderella had to admit that it felt like
that sometimes. But she tried not to think about it. It only really haunted her when she lay awake at night. During the day she kept herself so
busy that she didn't have time to dwell on the emptiness. And that flir-

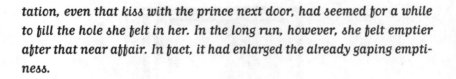

tation, even that kiss with the prince next door, had seemed for a while to fill the hole she felt in her. In the long run, however, she felt emptier after that near affair. In fact, it had enlarged the already gaping emptiness.

Cinderella sighed another of her patented sighs. Long and drawn out, it summed up the feelings turning her inside out. In the sigh were all the hopelessness, all the dashed dreams, and all the unfulfilled promises of her life. The therapist was right. She did have a hole in her soul.

Cinderella smiled at the memory of their first few days and weeks of marriage. She had been so content, and he had been so caring. It was perfect, and for those brief moments the hole had closed down; she could barely feel it. The emptiness had been filled, she thought. Wasn't that what was supposed to happen in fairy tales? When the handsome prince waltzes you out of your old existence and you fall in love with him, wasn't that supposed to fill the hole in your soul forever? Was it that she had married the wrong guy? Or had they just failed, no matter how hard they had tried at this thing called marriage? The questions were many, and the answers weren't forthcoming. But the nagging thought was there, growing insistently; if this was a real marriage, and if this was a good marriage, why didn't the emptiness go away?

Cinderella's question gets at the heart of what we have been talking about for the last nine chapters. We marry for many reasons, but I believe that underlying most of the things we have talked about so far is one simple and incredibly powerful motivation. We are seeking to fill the hole in our souls through a marriage relationship. (Larry Crabb's book, *Inside Out*, inspired much of the material in this chapter.) It may be true, in fact, that all of our attempts at human relationships come from this driving force. We feel an emptiness, a longing that, while we may keep it at bay for a time, always comes back, often larger and more insistently. What is this longing? What is this emptiness?

You and I are men and women who were created in the image of God. We were created for fellowship and an intimate relationship with God. But we are fallen creatures, and we live in a warped and fallen world. So all we can possibly do is know God imperfectly and incompletely. Although only God can fill the hole in our soul, on this side of heaven that happens only incompletely. So we look around for whatever else can fill that hole.

We are made for relationships. In fact, we are created for a perfect relationship with a holy and perfect God, who loves us as His children. But the warping of sin and disobedience have put us at odds with God, and even when we live forgiven lives, the gulf never completely goes away. It won't until we meet Him face-to-face. But we still feel that lack; we still feel that pain; and we still look for a way, any way, to fill it up.

Marriage Comes Closest

It is in a committed, mature marriage that we have the best chance of partially filling that hole. A mature marriage, free of the romantic expectations and the cultural craziness around falling in love, can at its best vaguely approximate God's love for us. After all, isn't that what God has commanded husbands to do? Husbands are to love their wives as Christ loved the church and gave Himself up for it.

Therefore, it makes sense that we look to marriage for a partial fulfillment of the hole in our souls. But we are coming at it from the wrong direction. It has to start with God. It is only in radiating the love and grace and mercy we receive from Him that we have a chance in our marriages. Listen closely. The agape, or unconditional love we receive from God isn't human, and we cannot create it within ourselves. It comes only from God. Our hope in our marriages is that at their best, we'll be able to share that love with our partners.

But when we look to our partners to create and originate that agape, unconditional love, they will fall short, and the yawning emptiness will grow larger. The best marriages are still only a shadow of the love that God has for us. And rarely are we at our best.

If you want to make your marriage a better place, the first thing to do is to work on your relationship with the God who made you and loves you. Ultimately our only hope, but certainly a valid hope, is that God's grace will wash over us and over our marriages. Without that grace, marriage can be very difficult. But when we exhibit that grace, that unmerited favor that God has bestowed on us, to our spouse, then something special and even beautiful can happen. Then we have a chance at real love. Then we have moved beyond the romantic ideals and the foolish hopes of our fantasies. When grace comes down and floods our life and washes clean our marriages, then something remarkable can happen. Marriage can echo God's love.

Avoiding Pain

The honesty it takes to admit what we just said is rare and only comes through the pain of real life. Most of us spend most of our time trying to avoid pain. It is why we don't acknowledge the hole in our souls. To acknowledge and lay claim to that emptiness is to give in to a truth we don't or can't admit. The truth is that life is hard. Although there is joy in the journey, it is a long and difficult road we face. And some of us, rather than acknowledge the reality of our pain, make every attempt to avoid it.

I heard a counselor once say that two-thirds of the people he sees in therapy are driven there because of their desire to avoid pain. If they would face the pain in their lives with honesty, much of their struggle would go away. Our marriages are one way we try to avoid pain. We want to anesthetize the pain. Our strongest anesthetic is our relationships. And our most important relationship is with our spouse.

God's Anesthetic

I do believe that our relationships with other human beings are what enable us to make it through life. I take to heart God's commandment to bear one another's burdens, and that is at the heart of friendship and marriage. While our marriage at its best makes our journey more joyful and takes the edge off some of the pain, like any anesthetic it doesn't deal with the real issue. And when we refuse to deal with the reality of our need for God and keep trying to make our marriages fit that hole, we are denying God His role, and we are creating enormous disappointment in our marriages. Your partner cannot fill the God-shaped hole in your soul. Many of us are like the toddler trying to make the square peg fit into the round hole. We figure if we just push hard enough, we can make it fit.

The desire to avoid pain leads us into all kinds of problems. It is where the romantic fantasy begins. It is where the desire for an affair starts. It is where our disillusionment and despair have their roots. The hole in your soul and the emptiness that haunts all of us in our more reflective moments aren't to be avoided, and that pain is best left undulled because it drives us to our Creator. It fills us with a longing for Him and His grace, and that is a very good thing.

Looking Forward

Again, the question is simple, yet profound. What do we need to do? In the last six chapters of this book we are going to present you with some choices you can make. In these choices you can choose to chase after a marriage that will never be—a romantic ideal that could never sustain the scrutiny of real life—or you can choose to build a mature and ultimately more fulfilling relationship. But to do that, you and I have to first acknowledge that we need God. Our marriage partner can become a solid friend and a needed resource on our life journey. Our marriage partner can help ease some of the pain and make the journey more joyful. But they will never replace the need we have for God. While our marriage can become a place of refuge in a fallen world, ultimately we have to love, not in the refuge but in the real world, because it is there that our journey begins and continues. It all has to start with God.

I was talking with a young woman not long ago who had left her husband. She had an affair, actually she had two or three affairs and in the end figured the marriage wasn't worth saving. Two years later, dry eyed and much wiser, her words rang with the wisdom of pain and failure. "I tried to make my own demons, my own inadequacies, my own struggles go away through my marriage. And when my husband couldn't do that for me, I looked elsewhere. But you know what, Jerry? It has to begin with God in my life. Without that, nothing else will work."

I agree. But don't look to God to take away the pain or the difficulty that drives you. God is not a cosmic painkiller. He isn't an aspirin to be taken at bedtime to make you and me feel better. We start with God because that is the only place to begin. We begin with God because He created us and knows us. And even though He has intimate knowledge of the darkness we hide from others, He still loves us and freely gives a grace that washes us clean every moment of our lives when we turn to Him. But the pain may still be there.

Turning your marriage over to God isn't going to change the fact that you may have married to escape or that your dreams and romantic fantasies have come to an end. God makes no promises to change our circumstances; the promise of God is that we never have to face them alone, for He is always with us, loving us and holding us.

Gwen became a Christian in her twenty-ninth year. Her marriage was tough. Her husband seemingly was unconcerned with her needs and her happiness. Well-meaning Christian friends told Gwen to "turn her marriage over to God" and let Him fix it. So Gwen did that. She prayed for her husband every day. She prayed for healing in her marriage every day. But nothing changed. Gwen is bitter and angry. She feels that God let her down and that He didn't keep His word. But Gwen has been misinformed, for God never promised to change others to make them meet our needs. Instead of praying for change in her husband, Gwen would have been wiser to pray for and actively work toward change in the one person she can control, and that is herself.

Pray, and Then Do

We aren't suggesting that you stop praying for your husband or your wife, or that it doesn't do any good to pray. Quite the contrary, in prayer we align ourselves more closely with God. In prayer we experience Him and learn what He asks of us. Only in prayer can we cry out with the emptiness and anguish in our lives. And God is there. But don't pray and then wait for a miracle. Pray and then work to change your marriage and your own life by making the kinds of choices that will make your marriage a better place.

It isn't God's responsibility to restore the passion to your marriage. Remember—God is much more concerned with your holiness than your happiness. It isn't God's responsibility to rekindle the romance. What

God has promised is to provide the strength to make the right choices when doing that is hard. God has promised that while our courage may flag and our will may fail, His does not.

So read the next six chapters of this book. You will not find the solution to the hole in your soul. Only meeting God in paradise will completely fill that void. You will not find ten steps to complete and utter joy in your marriage. If it were that easy, none of us would ever struggle in our marriages. You will not find a silver bullet or a magic wand. But readers who have made it this far into the book will find something of great value. The next six chapters will present you with amazing choices, and how you choose will determine whether your marriage grows into something that brings some joy and some measure of fulfillment into your life or whether it stays a struggle without an end.

If you're looking for your mate to meet all of your needs, to stir you with every glance, or to fill the emptiness in your soul, you need to go back and reread the first two parts of this book. But if you want something deeper, something that will stand the test of time, something that begins, even in a small and imperfect way, to reflect God's love for us, then you will find a map of sorts in the following pages, and you will find hope and help.

Filling the Hole in Your Soul

Instructions: This exercise introduces you to Scripture that talks about Jehovah God bringing satisfaction, fulfillment, and blessing to our lives. Although our sinful selves will never fully experience this, the Scripture is clear, satisfaction doesn't come from our mate or other earthly possessions, but from God. Carefully read the following Scripture and ask yourself the questions listed below.

Psalm 37:4	Psalm 90:14	Psalm 103:5
Psalm 145:17-19	Psalm 107:9	John 10:10
1 Timothy 6:17-19	Ephesians 1:3-8	

What does this passage say about satisfaction or fulfillment?

What is my part in receiving what God offers?

Am I honestly meeting God's requirements, when they are clear?

Am I somehow getting in the way of God's blessing on my life?

What changes does God desire of me?

CHAPTER 11

Cinderella's Choices

hat to do?" The thought had been haunting her for weeks, and even state dinners and new ball gowns couldn't chase it away. Cinderella was sick of her marriage. It hadn't turned out the way she wanted it to. It hadn't solved her problems. She almost missed scrubbing the floors for her stepmother. Yet when she really thought about him for long periods of time, she realized she still loved her Prince. But she didn't love him the same way anymore. It was as though they were roommates who shared chores. Actually, she felt more like an employee who had to accompany him on certain occasions. Whatever she called it, the spark was gone, and everything she had done to ignite it had not worked. She wanted out.

She could leave her Prince, the castle, and all of the nice things she now enjoyed, or she could stay and be miserable. These two options were not terribly attractive. The tears welled up yet again, and the pain and feel-

ings of being trapped pounded within, but the answer didn't come. What was she going to do?

Carol calmly laid out her clothes for the following morning, just as she had done for the previous fifteen years of her marriage. But tomorrow wouldn't be a day like any other. Tomorrow Carol would file for divorce. Tomorrow her family as she knew it would cease to be. Tomorrow her world would change. Crying softly at the enormity of the moment, she reached for the phone. She needed to talk to a friend, someone who would understand, someone who would tell her she was doing the right thing. She called an old friend who listened quietly, told her she was loved, and then asked the question that Carol had been asking herself all day: "Isn't there any other way for Jim and you to work out your difficulties?" It was a good question, but there wasn't a good answer.

Sandy looked at her husband in the near dark. He was sleeping peacefully. She wondered how he could do that. After any conflict, after the worst fight, he could just close his eyes and go to sleep. Not her. Sandy brooded and stewed on the words they had traded and over every raised eyebrow and sarcastic tone. Looking down at him now, she felt compassion for him, and she wanted the best for him, but it didn't feel much like love. She wanted to leave. She knew that he wanted to leave as well. But he was afraid of what the people from church would think and of what his family would say. She wasn't as worried about that, but she was concerned about the kids. She didn't relish the thought of being a single mom. It was just that the marriage was so dead. They had been to marriage seminars, and Sandy had read every book written on the subject, but nothing had worked. It was as if their love had just died.

But Sandy was committed. She wouldn't leave. She had remained true to her vows, and she wasn't going to quit. She just wondered if her only options were starting over again or living in a loveless marriage.

A Third Way

Cinderella, Carol, and Sandy are all in the same place, and like men and women around the world they see their choices in extremely stark terms. Risk leaving with all of the struggle and shame inherent in that, or stay and try to survive a loveless, empty marriage. It isn't hard to see why neither of those choices seem like very good options.

Some go...

Every week I talk to men and women who view their lives in exactly the same way. All they see is the choice to leave and start over again with someone else, or even alone. Their only real shot at happiness seems to be to get out, and many of them choose to do that. Unfortunately they find themselves in the same place three, four, or even ten years down the road. And when they leave, they add the failure of this relationship to the emotional baggage already weighing them down. Escape looks attractive, but it rarely works out the way they had planned.

Shirley told me of her own escape. How her first husband had left her, how she had left the second, and how she was looking to get out of her third marriage. In her words, "I didn't know it would be so hard. I kept thinking if I found the right person, it would all work out, but now I'm thinking the right person doesn't exist."

Some stay...

Wise men and women take notice of their friends' divorces, and some of them decide not to divorce out of loyalty or a sense of obligation or because of their values. Yet, although they decide to stay, they quit on their marriages. They stop trying to build something of value with their spouses, and they just exist. They build a life that is entirely separate, without anything approaching intimacy. They often become bitter and resentful. Just because they have managed to stay married doesn't put them in any better, or even different, place from the many who choose to leave.

Fred was a hardworking carpenter, very skilled with his hands, and he was known throughout town for his abilities. He looked at me bitterly and said, "OK, Jerry, I've stayed. I've lived with that woman for twenty-two years, and sixteen of them have been hell. I'm not going anywhere because I don't believe in divorce, but I tell you I don't like her, and I'm not obligated to do anything for her. I wish she would just stay out of my way."

Fred's words were harsh but they echoed the feelings of hundreds of men and women I have met who have chosen to remain married yet have quit on their marriages. Emotionally and spiritually they are separated. They just happen to share the same address.

Some find a better way...

People get married for all kinds of reasons. And we've tried to sort out some of them for you in the first few chapters of this book. People get divorced for all kinds of reasons as well. And people stay married for all kinds of reasons. We believe that too many people get divorced for the wrong reasons. They get out because they don't see any other alternatives. We think too many people stay in cold, empty marriages for the wrong reasons. Now don't get us wrong; we don't want them to get divorced. We just don't want them to quit on their marriages because they have no other choices. There is another way.

This other way is a hard road, and it requires the dedication and commitment of both partners, but ultimately it is the only road worth choosing. It isn't a path that promises complete happiness or complete intimacy, but it is the only road with any realistic chance for joy and fulfillment in your marriage. It isn't the path of roses and perfume, of never-ending romance and exciting sexuality, but it may be the only hope for real love. It is what we call the road of choices.

The Road of Choices

This road demands something very difficult from all of us; it demands that we face each and every day for the rest of our lives with our eyes wide open. It demands that we understand that each and every day we make choices that can make or break our relationship. It is a road that calls on us to make tough choices not once, or even six or seven times. This road of choices calls us to make good choices—unselfish choices— during each day. Then we have to do it all over again when the sun comes up tomorrow. In these choices we will find our share of love. In these choices we will find our share of intimacy. In these choices we will find joy. And down this road we will find a happy marriage.

One Couple's Story

"I married Dan because he wasn't like me. I wanted the structure, the plans he brought into my life. He was good with money; I was a disaster. He looked to the future; I thought tomorrow was a long way off. I think Dan saw in me the same thing—someone who would bring some flexibility to his regimented existence. He wanted some creativity in his carefully ordered world. It seemed like a good idea at the time.

"It wasn't a good idea at all. It wasn't long before I began to chafe under his budgets and his long-range plans. He became irritated and then angry at my inability to play by his carefully thought-out rules. He was a man of numbers; I was a woman of words, and we never seemed to talk the same language. I felt lonely, angry, and frustrated. I wanted out, but I wouldn't leave. It seemed less damaging to just try to stick it out. I guess I thought that it was better for two people to be miserable and unhappy than to make everyone else in the family miserable and unhappy. Divorce would just cause too much grief. Dan stayed with me because it was the right thing to do, but I don't think he liked me very much, and I'm certain he didn't respect me.

"We were so different. If I had a dollar for every time someone asked, 'How did you guys ever get together?' I could have bought a bookstore (Dan would have bought a bank). People assumed we had found some secret, but the truth was we just didn't tell anyone how unhappy we were. We went to church, we went to work, and we built almost entirely separate lives. And I think that is the way it would have remained, except something nearly miraculous happened.

"Dan and I went away to a marriage retreat. It wasn't my idea. I had long since given up on ever finding real happiness in my marriage. But the retreat was at a nice hotel, and work was getting stressful. It seemed like a nice break. So I went. After the morning session on the first day, we made an appointment to talk to one of the seminar leaders privately. Dan and I rather candidly discussed our differences. Honestly, we got a little heated even talking about them to another person. Dan wanted to minimize our struggles; I wanted to dramatize them. After pouring out our

lives, we weren't happy with each other. So it was with no little amaze-
ment that I noticed the seminar leader smiling. A laugh was beginning to
work its way out of his mouth. He thought our predicament was funny. I
was a little angry and hurt. It was my life, and I knew it was a little
messed up, but I didn't want ridicule.

"He didn't ridicule. Instead, he said something that began a change
that is still going on in our marriage to this day. He said, 'Why don't you
choose to look at your differences as an advantage? Why don't you see
how well you complement each other, and how well you two balance
each other out?'

"It doesn't sound especially profound to repeat it now, all these years
later, but it was a revolutionary idea to us. Again, to be honest it wasn't
me who made the effort. Dan started to ask my advice on some small matters. He even seemed to respect my opinion. That respect started something in me. I started to feel valued by Dan, and what used to bother him
about me now seemed to be viewed with a measure of thankfulness.

"Slowly my attitude toward Dan began to change. I began each day
thinking of the things I liked and valued about him. I made some choices
each and every day, choices to love and be faithful. Our struggles didn't
go away in a flash, but something remarkable had changed. We had chosen to love each other. And in that love was understanding, acceptance,
forgiveness, and obedience to God. At first the choices were hard, and it
was easy for me to go back to my own life and forget about Dan, but one
day I woke up and realized that I liked my husband and that he added
something tremendous to my life. That was four years after our marriage
retreat revelation.

"I don't want to suggest for a moment that we have arrived. Dan is
still a numbers guy, and I still speak in words. We still differ more than

we agree, but we have carved out a marriage I am proud of. And we did it by choosing the right things."

Karen

A Life of Your Choosing

We asked Karen to write her story because we think it illustrates better than anything we could have written about the power we have to shape our marriages. Any two people can create a marriage they can be proud of through the choices they make. What we decide every day matters. When you decide to forgive rather than hold a grudge against your partner, you are choosing for your marriage. When you choose to say no to that promising friendship with someone of the opposite sex because of the potential danger, you are choosing for your marriage. When you choose to stay engaged and connected rather than withdraw and protect yourself from pain, you are choosing for your marriage. When you choose to be honest about why you got married and the things that your marriage lacks and still stay, you are choosing for your marriage. When you give up on the fairy tale and see our cultural fantasy of romance for the hollow thing it is, you are choosing for your marriage. All of us can choose better, and all of us can choose well.

Judy's Story

I married for all the wrong reasons. I came from a needy and less than functional family. Jerry was a hoodlum and petty thief. We married without real faith. We started our life together as badly as anyone could. Yet we are still here thirty-three years later. And while it hasn't been fun every moment, when I look back at years that stretch my memory, I see mostly good times, and I feel a deep and rich satisfaction. This man and I have made it. And I love him. I love him even though he wasn't what I had hoped for. He loves me even though I don't measure up to his fairy tale. Somewhere along the line we decided to choose to stay married. And what we have learned about those choices make up the rest of this book.

Jerry and I were very different people with different gifts and different needs. Our first decision was to choose understanding. Since we were strong-willed and each of us was used to getting our own way, next we had to choose obedience (to God). Since we were tempted along the way by others who promised more than what we were getting from our spouses, we had to choose commitment. The fairy tale model didn't work for us. We weren't that one in a million love affair, and so to stay together we had to choose creativity. And after our children were gone, and we had done everything that couples were supposed to do, we had to choose to love all over again. We hope you make the same choices.

Choices Checklist

__Instructions:__ Carefully read the following statements. Check only those statements that are true for you.

___ I am aware that much of marriage involves choices I make.

___ I am ready to be responsible for my choices.

___ I am serious enough about my marriage to make the hard choices.

___ I am willing to stop an intimate friendship for the sake of my marriage.

___ I realize that my choices directly affect how I feel.

___ I understand that my choices have both positive and negative consequences for my marriage.

___ I am prepared to follow through on tough choices even when I don't feel like it.

___ I believe that God will honor my right choices.

CHAPTER 12

Choose Understanding

It was time for some clear choices. Cinderella understood that the time for wondering what to do was over. Whining and crying over what had gone before had to stop. It was time for her to make some decisions about her marriage and her prince. They didn't look like easy choices, and she wished to return to her fairy tale, but it was too late for the fantasy. She decided she wanted to fight for this marriage and for this man.

The royal marriage therapist had given her some very clear instructions: "Cinderella you are spending an enormous amount of energy worrying about yourself. Now I know that's what all your friends tell you to do, but I don't think it is helping you at all. I want you to try to see things from the Prince's perspective. Instead of leaving, I want you to choose to understand him, and when you begin to do that, love may return."

Five Things to Understand About Your Partner

Choosing understanding is the first step in building a marriage that can stand the test of time and the vagaries of our emotions. Choosing understanding requires a great deal of energy and commitment from us. It is important to know going in that when we embark on this less traveled road, it is a journey without an end. We never arrive. We will never understand our partner perfectly. And some of us may never even understand them imperfectly. (My wife is nodding her head as I write this. Evidently I am, at least according to her, difficult to figure out.) But all of us can take steps down this road; all of us can make a beginning on this journey.

Understand your partner's past

One of the sources of conflict Jerry and I had revolved around money. Actually the conflict was that he loved to spend money, and I worried that there wouldn't be enough of it. I struggled with Jerry's spending habits. I felt he spent money too easily, too often, and unnecessarily. I wanted desperately to have a savings account. I mean a real one that actually had more than $8.75 in it.

At the first church Jerry pastored (average Sunday attendance forty-two), there were many weeks that we would turn our paycheck back to the church because we knew they really couldn't afford to pay us. It was a difficult time for us financially. I remember one heated argument that seemed to have no resolution. Jerry just could not understand why I was so uptight about not having any money. In my anger and despair and our failure to understand each other, I shouted, "I don't want to be a poor widow like my mother!"

The light bulb went on for both of us. I was afraid that Jerry might die early as my father had. I did not want to repeat the struggles my mom went through after Dad died. Jerry understood for the first time. We talked about my past, and then he asked me what it would take to make me feel more secure. I said quickly, "$100,000." He smiled and said, "I will call the insurance agent tomorrow and take out an insurance policy for $100,000."

Judy's past experiences had influenced her greatly. Meanwhile, I had grown up in the home of a farmer. We were poor by today's standards, but even with seven kids there was always enough to eat. I never learned to worry about money. We always seemed to survive, and I thought and still think that if we just wait, everything will turn out all right. But Judy had known the insecurity of extreme poverty, and she had felt the shame of lack of clothes and nice things. She didn't want our children to feel the same way. She was afraid, and until I understood that, there was distance between us.

We talked at length earlier in this book about the influence of the past on our marriage. Unless you understand your partner's past and how it has affected him or her, you will never really know your partner. But when you choose to understand his or her past, much of the incomprehensible behavior begins to make sense and a reservoir of love and tolerance can overflow.

Looking at and even identifying with the past of our spouses gives us the opportunity to accept and understand their behavior and meet their needs. It could be a statement spoken to a child that was never forgotten (either positive or negative). It could be a special award or pat on the back that still means something after all these many years.

We often take on the fears and habits of our parents. My mother was very fearful and was always afraid of what people might say or think. I carried that into our marriage, and would say to Jerry, "What will people say?" His answer would always be, "So who cares what they think." When we discussed his flippant answer, Jerry said, "Judy, if you have been talked about and had stories told about you like I have, you would get used to it. You can't control what others say."

So how do you and I begin to gain some of that crucial understanding into our partner's past? It's really very simple. We ask our partner. Here are some key things that you and your spouse can discuss together:

Childhood and family. What was it like growing up in your family? What did you like? What did you dislike? What would you do different-ly? Did you have brothers and sisters? What were they like? Who was your favorite? Why? What was your mother like? What was your father like? How did they influence you? Whom do you most resemble? What good traits have you inherited from each of them? What negative traits? How might these (positive and negative) affect our relationship?

Traumatic experiences. What traumatic events occurred? How did they affect you? How did you work through the event? How does this affect you today?

Good times. Describe at least five positive experiences from your past. What happened? Who were you with? How did you feel? What made the experience memorable? Do you wish to repeat these experiences?

These questions are just a start, and you may have talked about these things when you first dated, but talk about them again and listen with an ear to understanding. It is OK to play amateur psychologist here if it helps you understand some basic cause-and-effect relationships in the life of your marriage partner (although I would be careful about prescribing solutions). Remember the idea is to understand, not to fix your partner's past or even to heal his or her memories. This isn't therapy; this is two people who need to understand each other if they are going to live together. This is about marriage survival.

Understand your partner's personality

I think some of our most exciting and meaningful times are the occasions Jerry and I take personality tests. And let me assure you, if there is a new test on the market, we will take it. Jerry is kind of a connoisseur of personality tests. (And yes, I know that's strange, but he seems to think it is normal.) It is also one way I can express my feelings in a cognitive way. While Jerry likes to be objective, I am very expressive and emotional. Testing shows this and gives us the opportunity to discuss it and realize that there is no wrong answer.

In 1983 we took our first TJTA test. Jerry scored at the 97th percentile on dominance; I scored at the 36th percentile. I laughed and pointed out how right I was when I said I never got my way. Interestingly, through the years our scores have changed. On our

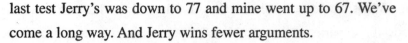

last test Jerry's was down to 77 and mine went up to 67. We've come a long way. And Jerry wins fewer arguments.

Early in our marriage I was frustrated by our lack of social life. I loved to party and be with friends. Jerry liked to fish or read. Big thrill! When we took another test, I was described as a "People Gatherer" and Jerry was a "Loner." Surprise, surprise, we have a source of conflict. After we discussed these findings, however, we understood each other better and were better able to consider the other person's needs. There was more give and take. Jerry realized one of the characteristics that drew him to me was my people gathering skills. He realized that was lacking in his life.

It isn't the method that has magic; it is the end result. We used personality tests because they helped us identify early on where we were very different and where we complemented each other. It is always fun for me when I lead our marriage prep classes through a basic personality test. Men and women who are planning on getting married and claim to know each other intimately are often surprised by the results of their tests. But realize that tests are only tools we use for achieving understanding, and there are many ways of accomplishing that.

Look at your husband or wife in social situations with a clear eye and, without making a value judgment, describe how he or she differs from you in conversation and body language. Don't do it to judge. Just observe the differences. You may learn a lot.

A Self-test

Answer the following questions about your partner and discuss together what difference it could make if you tend to be at one end of the continuum or the other. How might this affect your relationship? That is, how will you adapt to living with a person who scores high in pessimism, especially if you score high in optimism? Or, how will you adapt to a person who always wants to be around people, and you want to stay away from people as much as possible? What will that mean in everyday life?

The following questions are adapted from Taylor Johnson Temperament Analysis (TJTA) definitions published by Psychological Publications, Los Angeles, California. This instrument, used by many counselors and pastors, consists of 180 questions which measure nine concepts very well. Your pastor or counselor can administer and interpret this instrument. Judy and I take this test once every two or three years, and we always learn something new from it about our relationship. The following questions reflect the concepts measured by TJTA:

___Is your partner more tense and high strung or calm and relaxed?

___Is your partner more pessimistic or optimistic?

___Is your partner more socially involved or socially inactive?

___Is your partner more expressive or inhibited?

___Is your partner more compassionate or insensitive?

___Is your partner more emotional or rational and logical?

__Is your partner more assertive and competitive

or passive and compliant?

__Is your partner more critical and argumentative

or accepting and patient?

__Is your partner more controlled and organized

or changeable and disorganized?

When we understand our partners' personality, we begin to understand who they are and that helps us understand why they do what they do. The more we choose to understand who they are, and without judging their differences, the better our chance at intimacy and commitment.

Understand your partner's values

Most of us are value driven; that is, personal values cause us to conduct ourselves in certain ways. We do what brings us satisfaction and joy. We avoid things that aren't fun or cause us pain. We also make choices and decisions based on what we believe. All of us act out our values, and that is why in choosing to understand your partner's values it isn't that important what they say they believe. It is more important to watch what they actually live out.

For example, if I value recreation I will probably do that often. If my form of recreation is sailing and I live in Michigan, I will eagerly anticipate the sunny, windy days of summer. If I value snow skiing, I will get excited when I see the first snowflakes fall and start to think about my next ski trip. If I value politics and the political system, I may be very active in political circles. If I value religious teaching and ministry, I will most likely be active in a local church. The questions we need to ask ourselves are: What if my partner doesn't value the same things I do? Does that mean they will need to stop participating in those activities that reflect my values? Does that mean that I will need to learn to value the same things? How will we make the adjustments necessary to live together happily ever after? Tough questions. These are the kinds of things that can and often do tear marriages apart. But it doesn't have to be that way. It is possible for us to learn to value our partner's values and to see the influence and the power their values exert in their lives, even if we do not share every one of their values.

Milton Rokeach, researcher on values in the USA, created a neat little instrument, the Rokeach Value Survey, published by Consulting Psychologists Press, Palo Alto, California, which helps a person or couple rank thirty-six major values. This exercise can be the basis for a great discussion of personal values and how differences may be handled. Some of the items in this instrument are: An exciting life, family security, a comfortable life, true friendship, a world of beauty, loyalty, politeness, and honesty.

At the end of this chapter is an exercise adapted from the Rokeach Value Survey. Try to rank the items in order of importance to you, with 1 being most important. Have your partner do the same. Then compare and discuss your similarities and differences. This will give you an idea of the value of values and their significance in your relationship. We suggest that you purchase this instrument and complete the exercise in its entirety. It is available from the publisher noted on the previous page.

Another interesting exercise with this instrument is to rank the values as you would have answered ten years ago, or early in your relationship, and compare the results to your ranking today, noting the changes and movement in your life. You can also use this instrument to look at your ranking, especially the top five values, and to examine your life to see whether you are living out the values you ranked at the top. If you are, you are probably fulfilled and satisfied with your present state. If not, you may be somewhat unfulfilled and empty, lacking in direction and purpose. Consider making those changes that will better reflect your values as a couple.

The key here is not to get angry or disappointed with your partner when you value different things. The purpose is to foster understanding and build your marriage through understanding. Mari and Jason were a young couple who fought constantly. Although married for only two years, their life was becoming a continual verbal war. One of their recurring fights was over how they spent the little time they had for each other. Mari was always looking to go rock climbing or scuba diving, or even skydiving. She couldn't stand sitting around the house. Jason was more comfortable at home relaxing with his two or three best friends, watching a basketball game on TV and high-fiving each other following a spectacular dunk. When they took the complete values survey, they started by telling each other how wrong the other person was to value the things they did. But all of a sudden Mari said, "Look, don't you see; I value an exciting life. You place a higher value on friendship and comfort. I get it!" The light had gone on for Mari, and Jason got it as well. It wasn't that she was too hyper or that he was lazy; they just had different values.

Jason and Mari understood each other much better, but they also had to act on that understanding. They set up an informal schedule: Twice a month Mari picks the activities; twice a month Jason does. They have built a stronger friendship through that simple arrangement. They still fight too much, but they don't fight about this anymore.

Understand your partner's needs

Although we cannot assume the responsibility of meeting all of our partner's needs, we can and should attempt to meet some of them. The first step is knowing what those needs are. Some people's needs cry out to us and demand our attention. Others are not as recognizable, especially if our partner doesn't share them with us. In either case, all of us have certain needs that we expect our partner to meet. Some of these expectations are realistic; some are not. It doesn't matter. We have to know what those needs are, and if they aren't realistic, at least we can begin to deal with them. If they are realistic, then we can attempt to meet some of those needs. Without knowing our partner's needs, we will never reach understanding.

While needs differ greatly from person to person, everyone has core

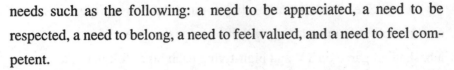

needs such as the following: a need to be appreciated, a need to be respected, a need to belong, a need to feel valued, and a need to feel competent.

Questions each of us need to answer are: What am I presently doing that blocks or hinders meeting my partner's needs? What am I presently doing that makes a valiant attempt to meet some of the above needs? How can I do better? How can I express appreciation to my partner? How can I demonstrate respect for my partner? How can I help my partner sense he or she is needed in the relationship? What can I do to help my spouse feel valued? How can I help my spouse have a sense of competency?

Write a list of ten answers for each of the questions above. Better yet, have your partner do this and then give it to you for your perusal and for discussion. I often use this exercise with clients who come into my office for counseling. It helps to have your partner list as many ways as possible for you to meet a particular need. Sometimes you may think you are meeting a need, but your partner doesn't pick up on it because he or she really doesn't want the need met your way. Such spouses want needs met their way. So look at your partner's list and decide to meet some of his or her needs in the ways your partner has suggested. Begin with the easy suggestions. Do the things you wouldn't really mind doing. Save the harder suggestions for a better day.

Understand their dreams

Jane walked into my office, sat down, and promptly burst into tears. She began to tell me about her marriage of less than two years. "I was so in love and so excited about marrying Jim. We couldn't wait to get married. We had so many dreams together. Now I'm so disappointed." I wondered what had happened. Had her husband left her? Was he involved with another woman? What was prompting the tears and the disillusion so obviously written across her face?

I asked Jane a simple question: "What happened? Can you pinpoint what is wrong in your marriage?"

"He's never home," she answered. "He works all the time, and when he does come home, he's tired. We never do anything together anymore. I thought when we got married, we would be together all the time and do all kinds of exciting things. He would never have to leave me again. Now it seems as though I never see him, and he seldom has time and energy for me. It's as though we're roommates, not lovers, not really even best friends. We never dream anymore. We just trudge on and on and on."

Sound familiar? Many couples begin their marriages full of dreams and expectations for their relationship. Too soon they settle into routines that kill their dreams and dull their relationships. Bills need to be paid, the yard needs mowing, meals need preparing, the house needs painting, and education needs to be completed. Children come along and with them an entire new set of duties and responsibilities that can drive us away from our spouse. And somehow in the middle of just surviving, frivolous things like dreams get set aside.

Couples need not settle for this disappointment. Routines, bills, housework, yard work, and children are all important parts of marriage, but they need not destroy our dreams or stop us from enjoying each other. In order to keep our marriages alive, we need to dream, together and separately. Mutual dreams keep excitement and anticipation alive in the marriage. Personal dreams keep us growing as individuals and make us more interesting people.

When you know and understand your partner's dreams, you are close to knowing your spouse on a very deep and profound level. Our hopes and dreams are what we are made of, and when we can honestly share those dreams with another person, we are really sharing ourselves. When we help our partners make their dreams come true, they become bigger people and our marriages become better.

Several years ago Judy gave me a little plaque with a sailboat on it. It is on my office wall. She said the words fit me: "Cherish yesterday, Dream tomorrow, Live today." It is difficult to cherish yesterday unless we live today. We cannot live to the fullest today apart from dreaming about tomorrow. When we allow ourselves to dream about tomorrow, we can live out those dreams today and then cherish the memories of yesterday. Without dreams, life does not seem quite so important or exciting. Marriages are made of stuff like this: dreaming, living, and cherishing memories.

We find fulfillment in our marriages as we help each other achieve our dreams. We build a strong friendship with our partners when we are daily working toward the fulfillment of mutual dreams. Marriages where couples aren't dreaming together can be dull, dry, and dead. It is in our dreams that we find hope for the future and reason to continue with the hard work of making a marriage successful.

Dreaming together is one of the best ways to affair-proof your marriage. If you and your partner have big plans and are working hard to make those plans come true, the excitement of another person in your partner's life just can't compete because you are already living out your dreams. You don't need to search for another with whom you can dream and fantasize. I once worked for a person who pulled me aside one day and strongly rebuked me. He said, "Schreur, you're always dreaming. You always want to make things better or different. You need to quit dreaming." After that conversation, I determined that I would not be long for that job. Within a year I was gone. "Quit dreaming" was like telling me to die. I want to live, and I want my marriage to live and grow and never die. As for me and my house, we will keep on dreaming.

Choosing understanding is never easy. In fact, it is often the hard road and difficult work. But it is the only chance we have to stay together and make our relationship with our husband or wife what God wants it to be. This isn't a magic wand, and there isn't any secret to be revealed, but the simple act of understanding changes marriages. If you and I make this choice, we have begun a journey toward a marriage that is whole and healthy, a marriage we can build on and be proud of, a marriage that isn't a fairy tale—but is something much better. We will then have a real life partner in our life journey, someone who truly understands and knows us.

My Needs and Values

Instructions: Rank the following needs and values according to their level of importance to you. Example: If "a need to be respected" is higher than all of the other needs, put a #1 in front of it. Go on to rank your #2 need, etc. Do the same with values.

Ranking my needs

__ A need to be appreciated

__ A need for companionship

__ A need to be respected

__ A need for recreation

__ A need to belong

__ A need for affection

__ A need to feel valued

__ A need for conversation

__ A need to feel competent

__ A need for sexual fulfillment

After completing this exercise, share the results with your partner. Compare results and discuss together how each of you might more fully meet the other's needs. Example: If my need is to be appreciated, how could my partner demonstrate appreciation? List ten ways they could do this. Allow them to choose various items from the list to demonstrate in future days and weeks. Periodically ask your partner how you are doing.

Ranking my values

___ Excitement   ___ Financial security

___ A comfortable life   ___ Close friendship

___ Beauty and art   ___ Loyalty

___ Politeness   ___ Integrity

___ Intelligence   ___ Service to others

___ Salvation   ___ Family

Other_____   Other_____

After completing this exercise share the results with your partner. Note similarities and differences. Discuss together how differences may affect your relationship. Ask yourself if you are living out the values as ranked, especially the top five. If not, decide whether these are your true values or not. If they are, but you are not living them out, think about how you could change your life to reflect the top values listed. Start immediately with changes to bring more consistency into your life.

Keep On Dreaming Checklist

Instructions: Please answer the following statements using this scale:

0 = Not Sure, 1 = Seldom, 2 = Sometimes, 3 = Often, 4 = Usually

1. ____ I feel free to dream about doing new things or going to new places.

2. ____ My partner feels free to dream big dreams.

3. ____ I work to make my dreams come true.

4. ____ I allow my partner to work toward fulfilling his/her dreams.

5. ____ I dream even when finances or circumstances seem opposed to any possibility of fulfillment.

6. ____ I encourage my partner to find and pursue new dreams.

7. ____ My partner believes in me and my dreams.

8. ____ My partner and I dream together.

____ Total Score

A score of 25–32 indicates that you and your partner are truly great dreamers. If you scored 17–24, you're doing OK, but an extra dream or two will help you. A score of less than 17 may indicate that you and your partner need more freedom to dream big dreams. Talk to your partner about your answers. If you answered "not sure" for your partner on #2, 4, 6, 7, 8, go to them and find out how they feel about that statement. Reread the part of the chapter on dreaming together and discuss how both of you could practice this together.

CHAPTER 13

Choose Obedience

◆━━━━━◦◦━━━━━◆

inderella didn't like being told what to do. Every time the minister opened his mouth in the royal chapel, she had a flashback to her stepmother leaning over her and pointing her finger, exclaiming, "Cinderella!" But she had to admit the preacher had a point. He was saying something about obeying God, and Cinderella believed that was an important thing to do.

Cinderella then heard something she hadn't heard in her entire life. "God loves you so much that He is less concerned with your happiness than He is with your holiness." In other words, how she felt mattered less than acting out of obedience to God. This was a new concept to Cinderella. She had always thought God's desire for her was to be happy. One of the thoughts that had occurred to her while she was struggling

with her choices in her marriage was that God never intended for her to
be unhappy. And if He wanted her happy, then obviously it would be OK
if she left, because that was the only way to be happy. This new bit of
knowledge, however, was like a bolt of lightning, and it changed her way
of thinking entirely.

Choosing understanding is difficult, but choosing to obey is even tougher. But it is an important step on that journey to an honest and growing marriage. It isn't about obeying our spouse and getting caught up in the arguments about who should run things in the family. It is about choosing to obey someone who is indisputably in a place of authority to tell us all what to do. It is about choosing to obey God.

Kent walked out on Kristin three days after their seventh anniversary. Things had been tough for a while in their marriage, and one day he just gave up. It was easier to move out than to deal with the wreck his marriage had become. Kristin was devastated, but she hadn't been happy either. She wanted Kent back, but she wanted her marriage to be something very different than the empty and cold thing it had become.

Kent agreed to see a counselor with Kristin, and as they sat in my office and discussed their differences and why they seemed to be headed for a divorce, Kent asked me a question: "Pastor, do you think leaving Kristin is the right thing to do?" It was a startling question, not because it didn't make sense, but because it makes all the sense in the world to ask the question, but it almost never happens. People headed for divorce talk about a lot of things, but right and wrong rarely enter the discussion.

I did something I often do in counseling; I let God speak for Himself. I opened the Bible and read a passage on marriage. Specifically I read the Ephesians passage, where husbands are told to love their wives as Christ loved the church. When I was done, Kent had tears in his eyes. "I want to do the right thing. Help me go back. Help me learn to live with my wife."

I wish more men like Kent made their way into my office, because he didn't need to be told to obey God. He just knew it was the right thing to do. And even though Kent knew it would be hard, he did it anyway, because it wasn't about his own happiness; it was about doing God's will.

I realize at this point I'm starting to sound like a tent revival preacher, but that's OK, because the simple truth is that our road to a whole marriage takes us into God's Word and His will. And without those things we don't stand a chance. Without obedience to God our marriages will never become what they can be. We have to put a stake in the ground somewhere and say, "This is what I believe, and I will obey no matter what happens."

There were times when I thought about leaving. I never entertained the thoughts for long because I was serious about God and my faith. Leaving Jerry never really became an option because every day I renewed my commitment to Jesus. And inherent in that commitment, no matter how badly I lived it out, was the commitment to obey God. So I obeyed and I stayed, and in that obedience I found true freedom, because I was doing what God wanted me to do. And, of course, I also found love.

Judy's words ring true because it is only in obedience that we find the freedom to love and create marriage the way God intended it to be. Only in obedience to Him is there hope for joy in this journey.

I talked with a young woman not long ago who was struggling with a tough marriage. She had married to escape a dysfunctional family, and although she had married a good man, they had little in common, and staying connected, even staying friends, was a difficult thing. We talked, and I asked her whether she was happy. Her reply surprised me with its wisdom. "Jerry, I don't look for happiness. It isn't a worthy goal, and it isn't something I think I could ever find if I did look for it. All I want to do is find some joy, and the only way I have ever been able to do that is by obeying my Creator. So that's what I do."

Choosing obedience doesn't mean giving up on happiness, but it does mean that we must recognize that happiness isn't the end all, be all. It isn't a worthy goal. It is an occasional oasis on the journey of life, but it isn't something to be sought. It happens with circumstances and with randomness. But joy, which is lasting and can infect a relationship, is found on the journey when we live in obedience to God.

Obedience in Communication

Obedience isn't just about staying in our marriages. That kind of obedience breeds martyrs with long faces who find no joy in their journey. It is about obeying God in at least two different and yet vital ways. We need to obey God in the way we communicate with each other.

I yell and scream. Well, not a lot, but when I get angry, I yell and I cry and I play the victim. Jerry gets real cold when he is angry. He gets very silent when he is upset or disappointed. Neither of these two different ways of handling communication has helped us deal with conflict. Neither of those things has helped us nurture our marriage. We talked past each other. Jerry would wait for my tirade to end and then walk away. I felt that he wasn't listening to me and didn't care. He felt that I was out of control. We didn't communicate the way God wanted us to.

Obedience in communication means that we move past our pet styles and the things that have worked to manipulate and served to control others for many years. It means we make a move to God's communication model. That model involves at least three things.

Communicate honestly

We are told by God to speak the truth in love. Some of us are afraid to tell the truth. We are afraid that the truth will hurt our partner or that the truth won't be forgiven. We are afraid that if we tell the truth, we won't be accepted. So we tell the easy lie instead, but this will not help our marriages.

Some of us hold the truth in for years. We keep from our partner all of our struggles and our problems. We hold back our disappointments and the things we don't like about them. And then one day, after years of storing it up, we breath fire on them and walk out of the marriage. That isn't what God had in mind.

God intertwines two concepts into His command to us. We are to be honest, but we are to express our honesty with love. The love softens the blow, and the love ensures we are telling the truth to benefit and nurture the other person.

Gene was excellent at telling the truth. He often told his wife how lousy she was and how disappointed he was. In truth he browbeat with his words, and every time he told her what she wasn't, she died a little bit inside. When I saw Gene, he was belligerent. For a man whose wife had just left, he seemed almost cocky. "I tell you this, Jerry. I never lied to her. If she can't take the truth, that's her problem. All I ever said to her was what she needed to hear."

I asked him a question: "How did your wife know you loved her? How did the truth get softened by love?"

"Oh, she knew. I mean I never cheated on her. Of course, I loved her."

I answered him, "All she knew was that you thought she was stupid and ugly. You thought she couldn't do anything right, and she never heard you say that you loved her. How is that speaking the truth in love?"

When we are honest in our communication, we build a bridge of trust, and when we are honest, we have a real chance to work out our differences. If we pretend that everything is OK when it's not, we aren't being honest, and we aren't doing our marriage any favors. God's model means we must speak the truth, even the frightening truth, even the truth about our misdeeds, and we must clothe those words in love.

Communicate positively

The Apostle Paul told the Christians in Ephesus to use words that build others up and don't tear them down (Eph. 4:29). Yet so much of our conversation is designed to build us up at the expense of others. Quite frankly, that isn't what God expects from us. We need to catch our partners doing something right and then tell him or her. We need to affirm our spouses and find things about them to appreciate. And for some of us that may take some thought. But if we affirm them, if we appreciate them, and if we express that to them, we will build strong marriages.

Our marriages are filled with husbands telling their wives what they don't like about them. Our homes are filled with wives who criticize and belittle their husbands. God's model doesn't tear others down so that we can feel superior. God asks us to build others up and to speak words of encouragement and comfort to them. Words that are positive.

Communicate with understanding

The goal of all communication is understanding. It isn't about making our point or being heard. It isn't about blowing off steam and giving someone a piece of our mind. It is about achieving understanding, and that is God's model. In the words of the prayer of Saint Francis, "Lord, grant that I may seek to understand rather than to be understood."

When we choose obedience, we choose to understand what our spouse is telling us. We choose to listen carefully. We choose to seek to understand rather than to seek to be understood. All of the talking in the world accomplishes nothing for your marriage until understanding is reached. Until your communication results in your partner's understanding what you are saying, your words are worthless, no matter how brilliant or well chosen they may seem to you. So seek understanding.

Obedience in Our Consideration

We show obedience by the ways we communicate. Moreover, the Apostle Peter also instructs us to be considerate of our spouses (1 Peter 3). Now that sounds like a pretty easy thing to do, but it isn't. Here's the good news: You can change your marriage for the better by enacting this simple principle. Listen to what God says about consideration, and our marriages will be radically different. We show consideration to our marriage partners by caring about them, respecting them, forgiving them, and affirming them.

Caring

Caring is simply empathic understanding. We obey God when we attempt to put ourselves in the shoes of our partners. We obey God when

we seek to see things from their point of view—when we try to literally feel their pain and their joy. Research on couples is very clear: When we communicate to our husbands and wives that we care, that we really do know what they are feeling, and that it matters to us, our marriages will be much better.

But that's the part that often gets left out. We care about our partners; we really do. We may even feel their pain, but we never communicate that to them. They don't know we care unless we tell them and we show them. Caring is a given in any growing marriage, but communicating that you care is tougher and happens less often. Take the time to show your partner that he or she matters to you. Listen to him or her, cry with him or her, and laugh with him or her. That is what empathic understanding is all about.

Respecting

When I talked to Marlene, she was headed out the door of her marriage. To listen to her tell the story, her husband, Dan, was an uncaring, unfeeling, selfish man. And in her words she was "sick and tired of it. It has just gone far enough." She wanted my blessing on her divorce. Needless to say, blessing divorces isn't the business I'm in. So we talked for the better part of an hour, and I encouraged her to come back with Dan. She didn't hold out much hope and was reluctant to even try, but she agreed to spend one session with Dan and me.

When Dan walked into the room, I was surprised. I had expected a large, even mountain of a man who intimidated his wife. But Dan was very short, a full five inches shorter than Marlene, and rail thin. To be honest he looked more like a nerdy college kid than a selfish, nearly abusive spouse. Appearances, however, certainly can be deceiving. Every word out of Dan's mouth was an attempt to belittle his wife. He belittled her job, her looks, and her family. It seemed that Dan had respect for only one person in the world, and that was himself. Marlene could never measure up.

As Dan talked, it became apparent that they were in deep trouble, and he realized he couldn't bully his wife in my office. She began to speak about how she had felt worthless for so many years, and no matter how hard she tried, it was never enough for her husband. Every time he opened his mouth to defend himself, she shut him back up with her tears and sincerity. She looked at him and said, "All I ever wanted was for you to respect me as a person, for who I am instead of for what I could do for you."

Dan learned something vital that day, something all of us who choose obedience need to know. When we choose obedience, we choose to respect our partner and to openly show that respect to them. The Bible tells both husbands and wives to respect each other. The Greek word that is used means to actually show reverence for each other. This means that we find qualities we admire in our spouses, and then we elevate them in our minds and in our actions because of those qualities. But it isn't about what they do; it is about who they are. We respect them for being, not just for doing. The doing flows out of the being, and too often we express ourselves only in terms of what they can do for us. If we choose obedience, we choose to respect our partner whom God has made.

One of the most profound needs all people have is the need to be respected by the people who know them best. And in reality, who knows us better than our husband or wife. Our partners crave our respect, and when they don't get it from us, their need may drive them to get it from other places and other people.

We need to ask our marriage partner how we can demonstrate respect for them. We need to ask them how our words show respect for them and how our deeds can demonstrate that respect. A marriage cannot grow and we cannot choose obedience without also choosing to show respect.

Affirming

It would be possible to write an entire book on the subject of affirmation. Let us simply say that choosing obedience means we choose to affirm our partners. We choose to look for the good qualities they have and the good things they do, and then tell them about it. It is not possible to overestimate the value of heartfelt and honest affirmation in a marriage. Your marriage cannot survive without affirmation. Affirmation and validation are closely related. Affirmation expresses and gives value to a person.

It is the one thing you can do today that will bring changes to your marriage tomorrow. You don't need a book or a counseling session. You and I need to simply walk into the room in which our marriage partner is sitting, excuse ourselves, and say, "Hey, I know I don't say it a lot, but I sure like the way you handle the kids. You are a good dad," or "You are a good mom. Thought you might want to know." And then without another word walk out of the room. Practice affirmation regularly and watch their guard drop and the walls come tumbling down. It isn't a magic wand, but it is remarkable what affirmation can do for your marriage.

Forgiving

When Wendy called me late one Thursday night and told me her husband Mark had confessed to an affair, I wasn't surprised. In working with them for nearly three months, their marriage and his actions had all the earmarks of an emotional involvement with another person. Tired of living in denial and ready to make an attempt to save his marriage, Mark had broken the news in a tear-filled evening that started with a romantic candlelight dinner and ended with recriminations and a very wounded wife.

When I next saw Mark and Wendy, he was a chastened man. He had broken off the relationship with the other woman, and he wanted to try again. But Wendy wouldn't let him. She felt betrayed, and she was angry—so angry that she wanted a divorce that would keep him from the kids and force him to sell his business. She wanted nothing less than to wreck him, emotionally and financially.

"Wendy," I began carefully, "your anger is appropriate. Your husband lied to you, and he broke his vows. Your pain is real, and it won't go away in a day or a week, or even in a matter of months. But whether you ultimately stay married or walk away, you are going to have to choose forgiveness if you want to be whole again. Because the bitterness that has already taken root in your soul will eat away at you until there is nothing left."

I didn't mean to be hard on her, but Wendy had lost sight of one of the most important things in a marriage. We need to choose forgiveness. If we have one shining example of anything from the Bible, it is the value of forgiveness. I remember a different couple: The man sat in my office and listened to his wife tell a tale of sexual addiction, of nights spent with nameless men, and of affairs literally too many to count. I watched this man in the months that followed take his wife into his arms, both of them sobbing with tears, and say, "I love you, and I forgive you. We will make it."

He wasn't in denial, and he wasn't glossing over the situation. The reality was way too stark for that. I asked him why he took her back. He looked at me, eyes shining. "Jerry, I remember reading a story in my Bible about Jesus and the disciples. When Jesus is asked about forgiveness, the disciples throw out what they think is a wild number, 'we would forgive someone seven times.' But that isn't even close to the forgiveness Jesus has for us and expects of us, for He said, 'Seventy times seven.' How could I not forgive my wife when I have been forgiven so much?"

When he was done speaking, the pain of her actions was written plainly on his face, and the betrayal and anger were there as well, but overshadowing it all was the tremendous grace that he was showing his wife.

When we choose obedience, we choose forgiveness. When we choose to be considerate, we are choosing to forgive, and not just once and not just when it is easy. We are choosing to forgive over and over again. All of us need forgiveness sooner or later because none of us is perfect. It may be a big thing like an affair or a series of seemingly inconsequential hurts and wounding, but every one of us will need to feel the cool water of grace from our partner. And when that water is an endless river that starts with God and flows through our marriage, then we have a chance to make our marriage work, even better than before.

And when we choose forgiveness, even when it seems like our partner doesn't deserve it, even when it seems as though he or she hasn't asked for it, we choose the way of the cross, the way of Jesus. And when we choose that path, we have chosen well.

The Bible & Obedience

Instructions: This exercise is somewhat different from the others. It is a miniature Bible study on the subject of obedience, especially as it relates to our relationship with our partner. Look up the biblical references listed below and write a short paraphrase for each biblical statement. Below each paraphrased statement write your personal response to that biblical truth.

John 14:15: My paraphrase of this verse:_____

My response to this biblical truth:_____

John 14:21: My paraphrase of this verse:_____

My response to this biblical truth:_____

1 John 2:3-5: My paraphrase of this verse:_____

My response to this biblical truth:_____

1 John 4:19-21: My paraphrase of this verse:_____

My response to this biblical truth:_____

Ephesians 4:29: My paraphrase of this verse:_____

My response to this biblical truth:_____

1 Peter 3:7: My paraphrase of this verse:_____

My response to this biblical truth:_____

1 Peter 1:14: My paraphrase of this verse:_____

My response to this biblical truth:_____

CHAPTER 14

Choose Commitment

$\mathfrak{I}$t all really comes to this," she thought, "either I choose to stay, with everything that means, or I choose to go." It wasn't a matter of pros and cons, of reasons, or even of emotions. She could think of many reasons to leave her Prince. She thought of all the fights lately, the coldness between them, the lies, and the mistrust. She even wondered if he was meeting another princess when he was off riding in the woods.

But at the end it was about choices. And, of course, she couldn't make a choice for him. She still longed for the romance, the times he had kissed her, and when it had sent a thrill through her like nothing she had ever felt before. But she knew now, it wasn't about those moments. It wasn't about the big palace or the finery that went with being a princess. It *came down to some simple choices, like it does for everybody, peasant or princess. At the end of the day there seemed to be so many reasons to go. The reasons to stay looked painfully inadequate—except for one thing, she had promised to stay, and maybe that was enough.*

Cinderella grasped the simple truth behind every marriage. At the end of the day the choice is stark, either stay or go. Every person who has been in a relationship with another person for longer than six months has plenty of reasons to go. When all of the failures and hurts are added up, the numbers may suggest leaving. When all of the faults and fights are put together, sometimes leaving appears to be the only good choice. We are people who are all too human, and we all make human mistakes. We sin, and we hurt each other. After a while it may seem that hurt is all there is. It is then that we choose to forget the apologies, to forget forgiveness, and to remember the bad instead of the good. And sometimes men and women choose to leave. And who can blame them? There is always a reason to go. At least, that is what we tell ourselves. But there also is a reason to stay.

We can choose to go down another path, more difficult, but infinitely more rewarding, the path that leads to joy. Choosing commitment is our only chance to break out of the cycle of trying to re-infatuate ourselves or the cycle of constantly needing someone new to thrill us and make us feel as if we are in love. Choosing commitment is the only real chance we have of building a marriage that we can be proud of, a marriage that brings a measure of love and satisfaction.

We live in a culture that mocks commitment and glorifies the moment. We live in a time when sacrifice is devalued and self-seeking is seen as a natural, if not particularly noble, goal. Choosing commitment when everyone around us is telling us to choose for ourselves, to have our immediate needs met, and to forgo the honor and power of a long lasting vow for the momentary thrill of an intimate moment, is a very difficult thing.

A series of relationships will not fill that hole in your soul. You can go from person to person, but the attraction will fade, the infatuation will end, and what is left will be yet another failure. Commitment is your only chance.

Commitment to Our Vows

It seems almost quaint, certainly provincial and definitely not very hip, to talk about the commitment we make when we utter our marriage vows. But it is with our vows that we make known our original commitment, and it is through those vows that we can begin to see where we may need to start with our renewed commitment.

Did those words mean something to you and me? Do the promises we made have any power over us now? Should they? When we choose commitment to our vows, we choose first and foremost to dedicate ourselves to doing what we said we would do. We choose to live up to the promises we made. And we choose to return to those promises after they have been broken and to remake them, attempting each time to live up to them.

When I married Jerry, I promised in sickness and in health, for richer and for poorer. I think Jerry didn't expect so much sickness, and I certainly wasn't prepared for so much poorer. When I made those vows, I never pictured the bad times. I never pictured our son in a hospital bed. I never pictured my illnesses. And I never pictured the paycheck that wouldn't stretch far enough no matter how hard we tried. I saw a fairy tale of roses and love, and

I assumed Jerry would take care of me. I assumed we would have our fairy tale, our romantic dream. But Jerry went to college after we were married, and then he pastored a small church. There just was never enough, and sometimes when I looked at my children wearing faded, hand-me-down clothes, I wondered why this was our lot. Then I remembered my vows, and although it sounds a little corny and maybe even a little pat, I realized that those words had power; they had the power of my promise in them. And my vows also included the tough times, and I continued to hang onto them.

Our vows are not just words we blithely utter in a ceremony of no significance. They are a promise, a promise we make before God and others. We have drifted away from the purpose of marriage ceremonies in this day and age. We see them as a celebration, and the ceremony is that, but it is not only that. Marriage ceremonies are moments of promise and accountability. We make promises, and we make them publicly. The idea behind a witness signing the marriage license is that we are held accountable for the promises we make. And it is in the living out of our vows that we find out what kind of people we are. It is in the choice to remember and be committed to our vows that we find out what we are really made of.

Men and women who choose commitment choose to remain true to their vows, and in time they learn the power of a promise kept. But what if those vows have been broken? What if one or both spouses have fallen short of the words spoken? Do we have an excuse to leave, maybe even a reason to do so? All of us fail to live up to both the letter and the spirit of our vows. There are times when we don't cherish, when we don't love, and when respect is gone and anger has taken its place. Broken vows aren't just about affairs and sexual liaisons. Remaining true to our vows is not about never falling short. It is about the commitment we make, tempered by grace and forgiveness, to keep our promises. The power of those promises can help us on our journey that has no end, our road to a whole and healthy marriage.

Commitment to Our Values

We choose to commit not only to the vows that we have made but also to the values that we hold. When we are lonely and our marriage has become a difficult place, our vows seem like promises made by another person in another life. It often takes more than that to keep us engaged in our marriage, to keep us from attending to the lure of another, and to bring us back after we have succumbed to that lure. As a matter of fact, sometimes when the vows have been broken and we feel permission to leave, it is our commitment to our values that holds the marriage together and allows for the promise of a brighter future.

Our values are what we believe. They are our ideals and what we aspire to live to. When we value a lifetime marriage, we value our faith and the example of a committed marriage to our children. Our values help us sort out right from wrong and help us determine whether we need to change our actions. When we remain committed to the values we claim, we give our marriage another chance to succeed.

When we act contrary to our values, whether that is by treating our husband or wife with disrespect, by failing to love our spouse, or by having an affair, we lessen ourselves. Whenever we act in opposition to what we hold to be true, we destroy a little piece of our self-esteem, and we become of less value in our own eyes. This becomes a destructive cycle as we continue in the affair or in the actions that we know are wrong. They make us feel bad about who we are, and then because we feel bad about who we are, it becomes easier to disrespect, to stop loving, or to look to another in an affair.

At some point we need to stop and look at ourselves—who we are and what we believe and how that should affect how we live. A friend of mine who had walked out on his wife and kids only to come back six months later told me why he returned and asked for forgiveness. "Jerry, my affair felt really good at one level. The sex was great. The woman was charming. And she made me feel great because she wanted to be with me. It boosted my ego. But at a deeper and far more important level I didn't like who I was becoming. I could feel the eyes of my children whenever I took the time to visit them. They weren't just disapproving; they were in shock. I was going directly contrary to what I had taught them. I was becoming somebody I didn't want to be. My values were still intact, but I wasn't living according to them. And I knew that God wasn't very happy with what I was doing. It soon became apparent that I either had to change my ideas of right and wrong, or I had to change my behavior. So I came home."

Scott came home in more ways than one. He made a return to the values that had served him well for so many years. He made a return to the God who had loved him faithfully. And in returning to those values, he returned to the commitment he had freely chosen when he made his vows to his wife so many years ago.

We all need to come home. We all need to make the choice to live out our values. We all need to choose to commit to doing the right thing. In that commitment there is the power of not just our will, but of God's grace, helping us to do the right thing.

Commitment to Our Virtues

We choose commitment to the vows we made. We commit to doing what we say we are going to do. We choose commitment to our values. We commit to live out our ideals and that which we aspire to. But we also must choose to commit to virtue—to building the qualities we need to become better husbands and wives.

When God talks about marriage in the Bible, His commands are rather simple. We are to mirror His love for us. And that means we need to live with virtues. We need to build some qualities into our lives. Quite simply, we need to make a commitment to becoming better people.

There is only one place to go for that model, and there is only one model worth following. We must commit ourselves to living as Christ would have us live—to emulate Him. My oldest son often tells the audiences he speaks to that as far as he is concerned the great bulk of what it means to live as a Christian is summed up in Ephesians 5:1-2: "Be imitators of God, therefore, as dearly loved children and live a life of love, just as Christ loved us and gave himself up for us as a fragrant offering and sacrifice to God."

I think Jack's words about summing up what it means to live Christianity need to be taken a step further. In these two verses we also have a picture of what it means to live in relationship with another person. When we commit to virtue, we are committing to becoming what God would have us to be, and in these two verses we learn exactly what God wants us to be. We are to exhibit the kind of love for our marriage partner that God has exhibited for us. We are to sacrifice for that person and serve him or her. If we practice these virtues, if we become "imitators of God," and if we even begin down that road, we will see miraculous changes in our marriages.

Commitment to a Person

It still may not be enough. We have our vows, but they seem to yellow and fade with age. We have our values, but they seem so much less important than our needs. We have our virtue, but that path is so steep and the climb so hard and long that we may give up. And then what is it that holds us to this marriage? You and I have made a commitment to a person—a living, breathing, changing, failing, loving, hurting, wounded, and wounding person. Ultimately it is to that person we must make and renew our commitment each day. We are not committed to our spouses because of what they can do for us or for what they bring to our lives. That will change with time and experience. We are not committed to them because they are so wonderful or special or any of that. There will come a time when we do not feel that way about our partner. We are committed to that person because he is our husband or she is our wife, and that is enough.

We choose to commit to our spouses for the same reason that God loves us, because they are of eternal value to God. We need to learn in so many small and seemingly inconsequential ways to see them as God sees them. They are not just flesh and sinew; they are souls—God's creation—and a promise to them is sacred, because this final act of creation by God is a sacred thing.

Commitment with Our Whole Heart

I talk to men and women every day who tell me they are committed to their marriage, but they are often holding something back. They refuse to give all they have because they are afraid of what that means. Instead, they commit to marriage—the idea or the concept, and they never make it a real, living, breathing commitment to the other person. This allows them to stay in the marriage but also to protect themselves by being disengaged from their marriage partner. That is not true commitment.

In true commitment we give it all: body, soul, and mind to the other person. That doesn't mean they run our lives or tell us what to do. It doesn't mean we become co-dependent. It means we do not withhold from them. We willingly give them everything we are, for that is the true nature of commitment

When you and your partner make that kind of commitment, you have created a relationship that will grow, because there are no stumbling blocks of deceit and mistrust. When you commit to your partner, you let him or her know you, and when your spouse knows you, all of you, then he or she can truly build a lasting and meaningful relationship with you. That is the way it works, and it is only through this commitment that we can continue down the road to a whole, healthy, grown-up, and potentially joyful marriage.

When I made my commitment, it was before God and all my family and friends. But the commitment I made was to a man, and that turned out to be both less and more than I had expected. He turned out to be a human being with frailties and fears just like me. He turned out to be cold and calculating sometimes, and wistful and romantic at others. He turned out to be both caring and unfeeling at times. He was, in short, just a man. But I had made a promise, a promise that seemed to be empty at times, but it was a promise I intended to keep. Sometimes that promise was easy to believe in, because times were good, and it was easy to be with Jerry and love him. But sometimes the promise was tough, and times were, too, and all I had were those words, my faith, and this all-too-human man.

As Cinderella also recognized at the beginning of this chapter, in the end it came to down to a choice to stay or to go. I chose to stay, and I had to make that choice many times over the years. I choose to love this man. Although I know him and see his faults and his strengths, nothing will cause me to give up on him and to give up on us.

Measuring Commitment Exercise

<u>Instructions</u>: Read the following statements carefully. Most of these statements are adapted from an audio tape by Howard Markman, *Fighting for Your Marriage*. Remember this is not a valid clinical instrument, but it does give some indication of the commitment level in your marriage. Please respond by using this scale:

**5 = Strongly Agree, 4 = Agree, 3 = Undecided,
2 = Disagree, 1 = Strongly Disagree**

___As I think about growing old, I am presently with the

person with whom I want to spend the rest of my life.

___I usually think of me and my partner as a team.

___Even when push comes to shove, our relationship sel-

dom takes a back seat to most other things in my life.

___I never spend time seriously thinking about what it would

be like to be with someone other than my partner.

___I am still willing to invest more time and energy into

building my relationship with my partner.

___I am strongly committed to helping my partner

become all that he or she can be, and demonstrating

that continually by unselfish actions.

___I have a strong desire to maintain and improve the

quality of our relationship and demonstrate that by

my actions and continual investment in our marriage.

___I will definitely continue in my marriage even through
difficult times.

___I am strongly committed to the continuation of our
marriage.

___I have many good reasons to stay in our marriage.

_____Total

Scoring: Total your scores. Scores will range from 10–50. A score of 40–50 indicates a high level of commitment to your marriage partner. If you scored between 30 and 39 you have a moderate level of commitment to your marriage partner. Scores of less than 30 indicate strong questions in your mind about your commitment to your partner and your marriage. You may want to talk to someone to discuss how to build more commitment to your marriage.

CHAPTER 15

Choose Creativity

The road ahead looked long for Cinderella. She was committed to her Prince. She wasn't going to leave. That wouldn't be fair to him. It wouldn't be right, and in the end she had decided it wouldn't even bring an end to her own longings. She was going to choose commitment. She was a believer, and she was also going to choose obedience. Even though it was tough, she was going to listen to the voice that called her from beyond the fairy tale and romantic ideal. She was going to obey that voice, and she was going to try to understand her Prince. After all, she wasn't the only one with a past. She had a wicked stepmother and some pretty brutal stepsisters. But it had to have been hard for him growing up in the castle with a father who was often busy and a mother who spent most of her time preening for the masses.

She decided to learn about her Prince anew, understand him, and hopefully, find a mature love.

What was troubling her today as she headed for her session with the royal marriage therapist was that it all seemed like so much work. It seemed as if there was no joy in the journey—only a nose-to-the-grindstone kind of tedium. She was committed. She wasn't going anywhere, but she hoped that there would be some fun and some joy—perhaps the therapist could point her in the right direction.

Many of the choices we make are tough ones. We choose commitment in the face of a desire to run away. We choose understanding when it is we who crave to be understood. We choose obedience when going our own way is much easier. We are afraid that after we do all of the right things, there will be no fun, and there will be nothing left but the hard work of staying married. That isn't necessarily the case. You can choose creativity. It's up to you.

Creativity is a vital component of any growing marriage. In choosing creativity, we add some of the excitement that the years have worn away. With creativity we don't try to re-infatuate ourselves, but rather we take what we have, look at it a bit differently, add something new, and together make something different and exciting. We try to keep growing and changing, and that too will make our marriages more interesting places to be. When we choose creativity, we choose a marriage that glows with life and laughter, a marriage that fills the difficult journey with joy. When we choose creativity, we aren't falling for the old romantic images that lead us only to disappointment. When we choose creativity, we aren't waiting for lightning to strike our relationships and rekindle a dying flame. When we choose creativity, we aren't relying on our fickle emotions or the chemistry of sexuality. When we choose creativity, we take responsibility to remake our lives and marriages. We choose to create, every day, a new, life-giving relationship. We choose to rediscover some zest for life.

It Isn't About Starting Over

You don't need to add entirely new ingredients to choose creativity. It isn't about beginning all over again. It involves taking what is already present in your relationship and enhancing it, making small changes that lead you into an entirely different kind of relationship. It is taking time with your partner to look at improving and re-mixing the old relationship. It isn't about throwing away what you have worked years to build, but taking the good stuff and making it better. It involves dreaming of how it could be and then taking the steps to make that happen. Choosing creativity involves at least three changes:

A change in perspective...

Choosing creativity means choosing to change your view of your relationship. That involves two key things. First of all, when we decide to change our perspective, we need to begin to accent the positive. Many of us are in the habit of finding what is wrong with our marriage partners. We spend a lot of time and energy letting them know exactly where they fall short. When we want to creatively rework our marriage, we start by looking for the good in our marriage and the good in our partner.

A friend of mine put it this way: "I realized that I had come to the place where I expected Sandy to annoy me. So I was looking for those things. It was as if I didn't expect to like her anymore. And besides, it was easier to blame her for the lack of feelings I had toward her. So I continued to look at her with a mixture of contempt and disgust. One day she stopped fighting back and told me, 'I can't ever please you. So why should I even try?' I thought about that for a while, and I started to notice little things she did well—like how good she was with the kids; how kind she was to me when I was overworked; and how she didn't complain about my parents (I complained about them all the time).

"I began to spend more time thinking about those qualities, and before I knew it, I liked her again. Together with the help of a counselor we began to look for the good things in our marriage. The poison that had seeped into our lives almost disappeared, and while I can't say it is the greatest marriage in the world, it sure seems to have a lot more possibilities than it did a few months ago."

Changing our perspective also involves something else, something that is key to creatively remaking our marriages. We need to reframe negative situations or negative character qualities. Reframing isn't tough. It means literally placing a new frame around the same picture. The frame changes the setting for the picture and gives it a different look. It doesn't change the picture itself. It changes the way we look at the picture, and it changes our interpretation and our perception of the picture.

Reframing is a key element in keeping some creative reworking in our marriage. You may have a hard time believing it, but Jerry isn't perfect, and some of his negative qualities really bother me. Instead of concentrating on the negative, I try to reframe it—look at it from a different perspective. One example should help clear up any misunderstanding. Jerry loves to spend money. Tomorrow is long time away for Jerry, but I think about it often and want to save for the future. We could, and have, in fact, argued long and hard about our differences in this area. But many years ago I began to see Jerry's spending habits differently. First, I noticed that he gave a lot of money away. So he wasn't irresponsible. In fact, he was rather generous. I also noticed how he liked to help people in small ways by taking them for dinner with us, buying a part for their car, and little things like that. So instead of seeing him as irresponsible, I began to admire his generosity to others. It literally changed the way I viewed him.

Judy and I could share story after story of how reframing has helped us. Reframing isn't a trick, and it doesn't mean we gloss over areas that need work. It does mean that we try to look at behaviors and situations in a new light, seeing the positive in them and then changing our perspective.

A change of paradigms...

In a very real way this entire book has been about changing our paradigm or our model of what a marriage ought to be. When we choose creativity, we choose to build our own model. It doesn't have to look like anyone else's marriage to work for us. It doesn't have to conform to our friends', families', or neighbors' ideas of what a marriage ought to be. It is your model and yours alone.

My son, Jon, and my daughter-in-law, Lynnette, have a marriage that works. In fact, it works very well. It is also an example of their creativity in building a marriage that works for them even if it doesn't look like our marriage or any other marriage I know. I don't know how many times Judy and I have looked at Jon and wondered, "How do they do it?" But they are happy, and they have creatively built a life that works for them.

Too many times we long for a marriage that never was—a golden time when we were blissfully happy and the real world never intruded on our marriage. The truth is that time probably never existed. You were never 100 percent intimate with your mate, but time has obscured the images of the past, and when you compare your life now with your life then, now seems wanting. But my guess is that it never was perfect, and yearning for a return to those days that never were doesn't help you and your partner build a better relationship in the here and now. And we need to be thankful for that.

We want our marriages to be fresh and exciting; that, after all, is what romance is supposed to be about. We can't promise romance, but when you shift your paradigm, when you throw out the old model of what a marriage was supposed to be, and when you create something new, you can find new excitement and satisfaction.

Dream with your partner about what your marriage would be like if you could build it from scratch. Leave out the romantic ideals and the fairy tale notions. Talk about how it really could be if everything you liked about it now was even better. Try to visualize the picture in your mind. Share that dream, and then work toward it together.

A change in practice

Be spontaneous, be flexible, play together, laugh often, and cry together. I feel like ending the book right here, because those are the hallmarks of a truly, realistic, intimate marriage. When you choose creativity, you are choosing a new way to relate. You are choosing to program for spontaneity. Sounds like a cliché, doesn't it? It isn't. What we mean is to allow time and a few dollars in your budget to run away to a campground or a hotel for the weekend. Allow time for a trip for ice cream and a bike ride through the house... yes, I said through the house. Be goofy once in a while, even if it isn't in your character. If you are a "by the book" type, throw out the book at least once a month and just have fun.

One of my favorite things to do in the world is to take the top off my car and go for a ride. I'll go anywhere as long as the sun is shining and the wind is in my hair. Judy is a different story. My granddaughter once said to her, "Grandma, your hair doesn't blow. It just lifts in sections." Judy cares about things like windblown hair. She cares about her appearance, and as a rule she doesn't like convertibles for that reason. But every once in a while she surprises me.

"Jerry, it's a beautiful day. Let's head out to the lakeshore and see Jack and the grandkids. And, Jerry, let's take the top off. It is just so beautiful." And then my wife lets her hair blow, and the sections lift, and we have great time, because she is being spontaneous. She knows how much I appreciate it.

Creativity in your marriage means being flexible. It means that you don't have to do things the way they have always been done. It means trying new things and doing old things differently. It means leaving the kids behind once in a while and taking them along once in a while. It means giving your spouse the freedom to create a life he or she can love and giving yourself the same freedom.

Play often and play hard. "How do you do it, Jerry?" It was a question from a close friend who knew that much of my life is spent with other people's problems. He said, "I would spend my whole life depressed if I had to hear the sad and awful stuff you contend with every day." He's right, of course. It isn't always fun counseling people. Often their stories and their struggles move me greatly. But Judy and I have a secret weapon to combat depression and boredom. We play hard.

Most of us don't play hard enough. We are too worried about our careers and not worried enough about our lives. We are too busy doing to enjoy being. Creative couples play together. And creative couples do not equate play with spending money. They walk on the beach, and they dance to their car radio in the parking lot as the sun goes down. They play when they get groceries. They ride the Ferris wheel, even when it costs $6.00!

Couples who choose creativity realize that without laughing and playing together they probably won't like each other very much. In a study of eighty college students, researchers found that intimacy motivation was positively associated with greater levels of laughter, smiling, and eye contact. Another study found that couples who laugh together stay together longer than those without this shared sense of humor. Humor enables us to cope, and it serves as an expression of pleasure, love, affection, and play. It promotes better interaction, imagination, and flexibility. Humor unites us and is a shortcut to closeness. One smile or laugh can communicate volumes. One of the most intimate things to do with your partner is to laugh with him or her. Some of our best times and closest moments are just sitting in our living room watching a funny movie and laughing together.

And if you don't spend time together, you probably won't do much laughing and playing together. Creative couples say no to important things so they can be together. A friend who runs a large corporation recently sent two members of his senior management team home. He said they needed to play with their families. Say no to extra hours at work, say no to extra jobs at church, say yes, at least once in a while, to sleeping in with your spouse, watching cartoons together on a Saturday morning, and watching infomercials late at night. Run barefoot through the wet grass, play in the rain, and catch a cold together. But take the time to do it.

If I had a dollar for every person who ever asked me how to restore the romance in his or her marriage, I would drive a faster, more expensive car. It is a question that we want answered because we crave romance. We love that feeling of being in love. We have already talked at length about how transitory that feeling is and how unworthy that goal is. But it can also be said that our best chance of developing a lifetime romance, minus the tingles which are never as thrilling as the romance novels, is through creativity.

When people say that romance is dead, what they often mean is that they are bored. They have fallen into a rut with their marriage and can't seem to pull themselves out of it. Creativity—creating a new kind of life—can destroy that kind of boredom. One couple I know got tired of their upper middle-class, lawyerly existence, left the practice, sold their condo, bought a sailboat, and sailed away. We visited and stayed with them on their boat in Florida recently. I asked Tim why they had done it. His answer was pretty simple: "Who wants to be a lawyer for the rest of his life?" Then he smiled and said, "No, really it was about finding some new things to do and just enjoying the simple life and each other."

That's pretty good advice. For joy in the journey requires that we choose creativity. That means changing our perspective of marriage. That includes accenting the positive, highlighting what is working in your marriage, and reframing the tough situations and negative qualities. It means creatively choosing to change your paradigm or your model of what a marriage should look like. The question shouldn't be: "What should our marriage be like?" The question should be: "What could our marriage be like?" Remember it is your marriage. It's up to you to make it what you want it to be. It isn't a matter of a capricious Cupid and his bow and arrow. It means changing your practices to help you build intimacy and increase satisfaction in your marriage. While it isn't a romance novel, doing new things and exploring new worlds will help you build a better, stronger, and mature love.

Choosing creativity isn't just for the naturally spontaneous or the artists among us. All of us can break free of long-practiced patterns and find new ways to live together. All of us, regardless of personality type, can learn new things. All of us can laugh at bad jokes and tell stories that can have us in stitches.

Don't use your personality or lack of creativity as an excuse. Ask anyone in my family, and they'll tell you I am not the creative type. As a matter of fact, my son, Jack, despairs when he tries to teach me about paintings and architecture—two of his loves, because frankly I don't get it. I also hate to play games, and I dislike parties. Yet Judy has succeeded in helping old rational me see the joy in spontaneity and the excitement of doing something I have never done before. It used to be unlike me to do those kinds of things. Now it is just the way I am. Thanks, Judy.

Choosing creativity is yet another step on that long journey toward a healthy marriage that gives us satisfaction and brings us a measure of joy. We know, because it has done that for us.

A New Way to View Your Partner

Instructions: Reframing a situation helps take the extreme out of the behavior and enables you to view your partner in a different way. The words we use to describe our partner can be perceived as either positive or negative. In reality we can use both negative and positive words to describe the same behavior or trait. For example, is your partner stingy or thrifty? Is your partner bossy or a leader?

Below are several examples of reframing. Use these to get you started with the process of reframing. For every negative trait or behavior of your partner, use another more positive word to describe that trait or behavior. Learn to view your partner more positively. A positive perception will lead to appreciation and respect for your partner rather than criticism and contempt.

Wastes money	Generous
Talks too much	Likes to share with others
Won't follow the rules	Creative/innovative
Picky, fussy	Attends to detail
Stubborn	Determined

A New Way to View Your Marriage

Instructions: This exercise will help to create a new picture of your marriage, a marriage that more accurately describes how you would like it to be. This exercise will not be easy because it involves two people, possibly two different views of the ideal marriage. However, if each of you will allow the other to dream a little and exercise some imagination, it is possible that the two of you could create a beautiful picture, which in time could become reality for you.

Create a new picture of your marriage relationship by following these suggestions:

Agree that this will not be an attempt to change your partner.

Allow your partner to dream a bit without discouragement from you.

List the items in the current picture that you would like to delete. Example: Every weekend we do the same thing, visit _____.

Make a list of other items that you would like to add to the picture. Example: I would like to make every holiday a long weekend in which we do something significant and fun.

Ask your partner to suggest one significant thing that you could do to make your life together more exciting. If it is humanly possible do it ASAP.

Ask yourself what you could do to make your life together more exciting. Do it immediately.

Think about friends whose marriages are a positive challenge to yours. What is different about their relationship? Could you emulate these differences? Ask them how they do it. Ask them to help you do the same.

A New Way to View Yourself

Instructions: This exercise will enable you to look at yourself differently and possibly make you a more interesting person, which will in turn enrich your marital relationship. The key to completing this exercise is the courage to act differently, even if it feels a bit awkward and uncomfortable for you.

Try a new look (outward) for yourself. A new hairstyle, some new and different clothes. Have a creative friend or one of your children help you make these choices.

Be less predictable and more spontaneous. When your partner makes a suggestion, don't even think about it, do it. When you think of something, jump into it with both feet (unless it causes you to go bankrupt, of course).

Be more playful, laugh more. Determine not to be so serious about everything. Start with not taking yourself so seriously. Read joke books together.

Surprise your partner with a weekend away or a special night together at a nice place. Don't ask them, just do it. If you are on the receiving end, go for it and enjoy the experience. Don't pour cold water on your partner's innovation and creativity.

Do something totally out of character for you. Don't worry what others will think. Just do it. If your partner does this, don't rebuke him or her, just enjoy the experience.

Be open to new experiences. This may involve a little risk, but usually it is worth it and will give you something to talk about and remember for years to come. Example: Go snorkeling or para-sailing, or learn a new hobby.

If you are bored with your job, look for another one, or if your career is going nowhere, think about going a different direction, a direction that you always wanted to take.

Treat yourself on a regular basis. Celebrate small things. Reward yourself for a job well done.

Serve others. Get involved in a ministry at your place of worship. Do something significant for another person, without looking for anything in return.

Make a fresh commitment to love Jesus with your whole heart and soul. Determine to live for Him every day. (After all, He died for you).

CHAPTER 16

Choose Love

He swept her into his arms and carried her across the threshold. Their lovemaking was both powerful and sweet. Cinderella's memories of that first night with Prince Charming were beginning to fade a bit around the edges. But she still remembered how safe she had felt in his arms that night. She still remembered feeling, for the first time in a long time, as if she belonged and had a place. She smiled at the memory of her fairy godmother. "Where are you when I really need you?" she thought out loud. But evidently fairy godmothers that waved magic wands were for the fairy tale, and when the fairy tale ended and real life began, Cinderella was on her own.

The memories of that first night of the romance and the glamour of marrying her Prince helped Cinderella when real life was boring and the Prince was off slaying a dragon somewhere far away. But Cinderella was determined that although her fairy tale had ended, her marriage would not. She had made some tough choices. She had determined to do her part to create a marriage, a family she could be proud of. And last night after they had made love for the first time in a long time, she had begun the process with her Prince.

Lying in his arms, she asked him, "Honey, do you feel alone and afraid sometimes? Do you feel distant from me, as though we're drifting apart?" It must have seemed an odd question for the Prince, following as it did their making love, but he knew what Cinderella was talking about. He, too, had felt the pull of another woman. He had felt the fire die in their marriage. Yet he didn't want to lose her. They talked deep into the night, and the last question she asked him, following their mutual commitment to love each other through good times and bad, was: "What is it you want our marriage to be?" And then she fell asleep, and that question would have to be answered each new day with the dawning of the sun.

The Choices We Make

The last few chapters have dealt with the choices we must make if we want to build a lasting, honest marriage that will stand the test of time. Some of those choices are hard, requiring some self-denial and some will. Some of them are fun choices, choosing to love and to play together. But what we have asked throughout this book is that you make some very difficult choices. We have asked you to give up the notion that in your marriage you will be able to complete yourself. We have asked you to give up the notion that in this marriage you will be able to fill the hole in your soul. We have asked you to become realistic about romance. We have, in fact, asked a lot.

But we asked that of you for one simple reason. Only by letting go of the fantasy, can you grab hold of something more vital, more powerful, and infinitely more satisfying. Only when you realize that you are marrying a human being who brings as much or more pain and unfinished business into the relationship as you do, can you begin to create something that will become very special. We have asked that you forgo your illusions, because it is really your only chance at real joy and fulfillment.

Looking back, I guess we never should have made it. How do an eighteen-year-old, pregnant bride and a twenty-two-year-old, convicted felon manage to stay married for thirty-three years? We did everything wrong. We got married for the wrong reasons. We got married out of need and anger and pain and difficulty and lust and yes, even love. But we had no faith in God and very little faith in each other. I went into marriage looking for someone to take my dead father's place, taking care of me and telling me I was valuable. I married a man who expected me to take care of myself and wasn't very good at expressing his feelings. How have we managed not only to survive together, but also to find more than our measure of joy and peace?

The only answer that I have is that God has washed our marriage in His grace and mercy. It sounds like the "churchy" thing to say, but without God's love we wouldn't be where we are today. Without an everyday grace that enabled us to forgive each other and to love each other, knowing that neither of us deserved it, well, I think I would have quit a long time ago.

I have one thing to say, for anyone who wants to know if staying is worth it and if making it through the difficult times has any value at the end. The answer to your questions is yes. I look at Jerry so differently than I used to. In some ways he hasn't changed very much, but in the ways that really matter he has become an entirely new person. I can see him as I write these words: His hair is gray, and his stomach isn't as flat as it once was. He moves a little slower, but drives almost as fast. He reads more and listens more, and I think he loves me more. He certainly tells me more. But the changes I'm most surprised by aren't in his life. They are in mine. I've become so different. I struggled so hard to find myself and to build an identity. I've struggled with my faith, and I've worried endlessly about my kids. Through it all Jerry has been there. And he has loved me.

Is it worth it? Yes, for we are a couple; we are partners; we live together; and we have created a life that brings us no small measure of joy and even delight. I love him, and I am glad I stayed.

A Reflection of Grace

At its best, marriage reflects the grace of God in our lives. At its best, marriage teaches us about the way God loves us. At its best, marriage palely imitates God's love for us. At its best, marriage is not enough. We still need God. And, of course, without God our marriages will never be at their best. It just isn't possible to love fully without acknowledging that we are fully loved by the One who created us and sustains us.

So that is where any marriage renewal must start. It must begin with yet another, all-important choice. If we are to choose for our marriage, we must choose first for God. We must choose, in the words of Brennan Manning, to "live in the accepted love of Jesus." That is the beginning of life, indeed, all real life. Only by first choosing to be loved by God can we ever choose to love another human being. It all starts with the One who created us.

A Higher Love

I believe that when we look to our marriages and look for someone to share our lives with, we are searching for a higher love. We are searching for a love that will put to rest our longings and our pain. We are searching for a healing of the hole that rends our souls and breaks our spirits. We find someone who cares, and for a brief moment we fill that hole, but then the moment passes, and we are left with a real person—a husband, a wife, and a hole that still cries for more. Have we missed that higher love? Have we married the wrong person?

I don't think so. I think we still have a chance at that higher love, never completely, for that only happens in heaven when we are with our Heavenly Father. But we have a chance to lift our commonplace lives and make them richer. We have a chance to mend our broken vows and make them whole. We have a chance to lift our wounded spirits and feel the beginning of healing. We have that chance when we choose to let God's love flow through us and into our marriage, our children, our husband, or our wife. And then in response to God's grace on us, we come together as partners and as a couple and say thank-you to the God who has lifted us. It can happen, but never without Him.

Your Life, Your Choices, His Plan

It is your life. And God does not force your choices. He leaves them for you to make; that too is an expression of His grace. He doesn't promise you and me happiness. He makes no pretense that it will always be easy when we follow Him. He doesn't tell us that He will make our wives more caring or our husbands more faithful. He will not wipe away all the damage that has been done to us by others. We are still, at least in part, products of our past. And there is no guarantee that if you choose for your marriage, it will become all you hope it could be.

But listen well—only in choosing to let God love us do we have the opportunity to participate in His plan for building joy and meaning into our marriages. So let us end this book with three challenges—one for those who have yet to marry, one for those who have married, and one for those who no longer want to be married.

Before you start

If you are reading this book and your wedding is planned, the flowers have been ordered, the dress has been altered, and the invitations are at the printers, you may be feeling a little overwhelmed. This book is honest and unflinching in its portrayals of the difficulties you will face in your marriage. But don't despair. We love marriage and believe that you can find joy and meaning in your lifetime commitment to another human being.

Before you start, read this book together, and then decide if you are capable and ready to make the choices you will have to make to build a lifetime marriage. Don't gloss over the differences in your lives, and don't read the stories in this book thinking they happen only to other people. You, my friends, are "other people," and they can happen to you. So start out your marriage by making these tough choices. Start first and foremost by choosing to let God's grace overwhelm you and flow through your life.

Use all the resources available to help you get started right. Most churches now offer marriage preparation courses. Your pastor or counselor can be of tremendous help to you. Another older couple also could be your mentor and help you avoid some of the problems they encountered in their marriage.

In the middle

You have been married for four, five, or fifteen years, and the romance has gone. You still love your partner, but you are beginning to wonder if this is all there is, and when the house is quiet, you wonder if you have missed out on something. Before things get worse, take a weekend with your partner, tell your partner how you feel, and work through some of the exercises in this book. Look at your marriage creatively, and dream together, making your marriage a thing of beauty for you.

Don't wait until you both feel despair and only anger and disappointment are left. Begin to make a marriage that breaks the mold today. Take the time to consider your choices, and then with your partner choose for your marriage. You will save yourself the pain that many people have gone through if you make those choices now before the damage has been done.

Do one more small thing. Begin to thank God every day for your partner, finding in him or her things that you admire and love. And then tell both God and your partner about what you have found.

On the way out

You picked up this book because you are at the end of your rope. Your marriage has become a suffocating, painful thing, and the only way you think you can survive is to escape. You picked up this book hoping against hope for some kind of formula that would fix what is broken. Maybe it was your last try at staying. Maybe your husband or your wife handed you this book, and you read it defiantly—your mind already made up.

For you, we have one message. Wherever you go, you take yourself with you. What we mean is that you will not escape your problems when you leave. You will not quiet the pain in your soul. It may subside for a while, and in an affair you may even hear your own heart pounding loud enough to drown out the cry of your spirit, but not for long. We urge you to start by finding a Christian counselor and telling him or her the truth. All of the truth. Whatever lies and deceit have crept into your life, whatever you have hidden in order to protect yourself, share them with your counselor. And then with the help of that counselor, tell your partner.

We could tell you to stay, and leave it at that, but that is your choice. We will tell you that to leave without ever choosing to let God's grace flow through your marriage and to leave without ever really choosing for your marriage will not take away the pain; it will only add to it. Seek help, and pray for hope.

We Believe

Judy and I have been married for thirty-three years. We have not always been happy; we have often disagreed. We have argued and hurt each other. We have said things we instantly wished we could have taken back. And for a couple who's supposed to know a lot about marriage, it still seems as though we have a long way to go—even after thirty-three years!

We have found love through those hurts and those years. We have discovered something through the laughter and the tears. When we choose to let God's love flow through us, we have found a joy in our shared journey. We have left the fairy tale behind long ago, and romance, while fun, isn't really our concern. We are looking for that higher love.

I don't know how many years are left for us in this world. I don't know what God will choose to do with us in the remaining years. I do know this: I choose to spend those years, moment by moment, with this woman. I love her, and I couldn't dream of living any other way. We believe that it is possible to keep the "happily" in ever after.

And now I will show you the most excellent way. If I speak in the tongues of men and of angels, but have not love, I am only a resounding gong or a clanging cymbal. If I have the gift of prophecy and can fathom all mysteries and all knowledge, and if I have a faith that can move mountains, but have not love, I am nothing. If I give all I possess to the poor and surrender my body to the flames, but have not love, I gain nothing. Love is patient, love is kind. It does not envy, it does not boast, it is not proud. It is not rude, it is not self-seeking, it is not easily angered, it keeps no record of wrongs. Love does not delight in evil but rejoices with the truth. It always protects, always trusts, always hopes, always perseveres. Love never fails (1 Cor. 13:1-8).